Arroyo Center

ALGERIA

THE NEXT FUNDAMENTALIST STATE?

GRAHAM E. FULLER

Prepared for the
United States Army

RAND

PREFACE

This study is part of a series of studies the author has written for RAND on the subject of Islamic fundamentalism, or Islamism, in the Muslim world. This study is of particular policy importance since it deals with the prospect of a fundamentalist victory in the largest and one of the most important Arab states—Algeria. An Islamist regime in Algeria would have major repercussions in the region. This study attempts to put such a takeover in perspective: Why might it happen, what would it look like, and what would it mean for the West and the region? This problem is of interest not only to Washington but even more to Western Europe, which is already the recipient of many North African immigrants, threatened by potential refugee flows, and increasingly dependent upon Algerian natural gas. The study also attempts to look at the Algerian case on a comparative basis: How does the Algerian experience contribute to our knowledge of the varieties of political Islam as a broader regional phenomenon?

This research was sponsored by the Deputy Chief of Staff for Operations (DAMO-SSP) and performed within the Strategy and Doctrine Program of RAND's Arroyo Center, a federally funded research and development center sponsored by the United States Army.

CONTENTS

SUMMARY

Algeria is in agony, caught up in a four-year paralyzing spiral of violence that has almost brought the state to its knees. Its ruling junta lacks legitimacy; its November 1995 "presidential elections" excluded representatives of almost all the leading political parties of the country, including the powerful Islamist FIS. The deep civil conflict cannot be resolved and the nation returned to normalcy until genuine parliamentary elections are held in which all significant political parties are represented. The regime seems determined to reject parliamentary elections as long as the FIS stands a chance of gaining a dominant—or even major—voice in the government. Yet the FIS cannot be excluded if national and social reconciliation is to come about. President Liamin Zerwal faces the formidable task of moving his country toward national elections but may be unable, or unwilling, to do so. If he does not, Algeria remains condemned to continuing widespread violence, paralysis, and radicalization of its political forces.

The West needs to ensure that this important country on southern Europe's doorstep moves gradually toward reconciliation via elections that cannot exclude the FIS—the biggest single winner in the annulled 1991 elections. A potentially major FIS voice in government does carry risks, but the alternatives are worse. A FIS government may be uncongenial to the West but is unlikely to fundamentally threaten Western interests; if *legally* elected, it will be under strong constraints to leave power if not reelected for a second term—as it has promised to do.

*   *   *

One of the largest and most important states in the Arab world is in a state of virtual civil war. Algeria has become the battleground of a massive ideological struggle pitting conflicting legacies and visions of the future against each other. It is fashionable, and perhaps reassuring to Westerners, to picture the scene in terms of modernism contesting with reactionary or medieval forces. This simplistic vision does not conform with a more complicated reality that involves issues of democracy versus authoritarianism, a challenge to a corrupt and failed elitist rule, the search for cultural and political "authenticity," class struggle, a European versus an Arab orientation, generational differences, the imperialist legacy, and a huge debate over what it is to be "modern." Between the present regime and its Islamist opponents, there are no obvious champions of a "right" cause with whom Westerners can feel comfortable.

THE SOURCE OF FIS STRENGTH

The Algerian "fundamentalist" movement, the Islamic Salvation Front (FIS in French), is likely to gain a major voice in the power equation of the Algerian state within the next few years—although not necessarily absolute power. The existing regime—basically a military junta—is intellectually and politically bankrupt; the country is racked by the bloody beginnings of what could yet be full-scale civil war. The current ruling junta—reaping the legacy of years of mismanagement and strict authoritarian control by the army and its National Liberation Front (FLN in French) that had ruled the country since independence in 1962—has no effective answers to Algeria's present crisis except to hold onto power through force and hope for better times. Hard-line military officers at the top of the system are adamant about excluding the FIS from power at all costs, and will pursue only a military option to defeat it.

The FIS is the single strongest and most popular political alternative in the country, and it has already won a clear plurality in Algeria's first and only free national elections in late 1991—only to see the results annulled by the army. Today it would almost certainly win a plurality again, if not a slim majority. The FIS has strong ties with the grass roots of the population, and understands mass grievances better than almost any other party, especially among the urban poor, lower middle class, and marginalized educated class—all of which lack housing, jobs, and social services—the legacy of decades of FLN misrule. Despite a FIS grasp of what is wrong with the nation and a high degree of neighborhood social activism, like many other Islamist movements in other countries, it purveys a message rather long on abstract principles, short on details, and fond of the slogan that "Islam is the answer."

Although political violence had been relatively limited before the late 1991 elections, the FIS felt compelled to turn to it following the military's annulment of the election results and the subsequent eradication of the party as a political entity by force and massive arrests. Since early 1992, the spiral of violence has risen dramatically—as much as 50,000 dead on both sides in a brutal and bloody confrontation. It will be difficult to stop the logic of events that is leading to the government's increasing marginalization, loss of support, and eventual collapse.

The FIS had had a year or two experience of power, at the municipal level in various cities in Algeria in 1990–1991, in which it was neither especially radical nor especially effective. Today, while decrying the clear defects of the Algerian state and society, the FIS has no clearcut program of action on national problems, other than some general principles that are unclear in their specific policy implications. It is seriously divided internally, between radicals and moderates, and about what policies to adopt. Three years of sustained and brutal violence in clashes between the government and the FIS have polarized the country, strengthening radical forces within the FIS, reinforcing hard-liners within the regime, and spawning a number of dangerous, independent, militant armed radical groups operating outside of FIS control.

FIS ROOTS IN ALGERIAN POLITICAL CULTURE

While the FIS represents a seemingly radical alternative to the old ruling National Liberation Front (FLN), in many ways the FIS actually shares many important qualities with the FLN—in psychological outlook and political culture. The FIS, in power, is likely to reflect a great deal more about Algeria than about Islam:

- Algerian political culture includes powerful elements of xenophobia, born especially of 130 years of colonialism (including millions of French colons then living in Algeria), and a long, brutal, and bloody struggle against the French for an independence that was attained only as late as 1962.

- Algeria—itself one of the major symbols of anticolonial struggle as powerful as Vietnam—since independence has been deeply involved in the Third World movement, complete with a strong antiimperialist ideology and a tradition of strong support for other Third World radical movements in Cuba, South Africa, Vietnam, Mozambique, etc. It has maintained a sense of mission toward international struggle—even if sobered by its own problems over the last decade and showing increasing pragmatism.

- Algeria has a long tradition of state socialism, the most intense in the Arab world.

- As a postcolonial culture, the country nourishes deep anti-French currents (but with a touch of ambivalence), is fiercely independent-minded, and extremely prickly toward the outside world.

- It has a tradition of suspicion of the outside world in general, of the international political order it sees dominated by great Western powers, and of the international economic order, which it sees as rigged against the interests of the Third World. Algeria tends to be austere and egalitarian as a political culture.

- Algeria, despite its socialist outlook, has always included Islam as a basic element of its political creed and national identity.

- But it also has a tradition of realism and sober-mindedness, even while pursuing a more radical foreign policy. It has a history of honoring legality and negotiation, even while adopting radical positions in that context. Since independence, it has not employed international terror in support of radical national goals.

- It has been engaged in an ongoing search for national identity, never having constituted a clear-cut historical region until the era of French colonialism (unlike Morocco and Tunisia, which have very well established identities going back over a thousand years). The search for Algerian identity has especially invoked Arabic and Arab nationalism. Yet the Algerian identity is also Franco-Mediterranean and Berber—20 percent of the population speak Berber and perhaps 75 percent of the population are Berber in blood, although now fully Arabized.

It is almost certain that Algeria will continue to demonstrate most of these same qualities under any future FIS rule, to one extent or another.

CONJECTURES ON THE FIS IN POWER

It is impossible to predict with any certainty the policies of the FIS in power; its behavior will depend greatly upon the precise conditions under which it comes to power, and the specific personalities that emerge on top. In general, the longer the bloody struggle with the state goes on, the more radicalized the FIS will likely become. But based on what is known about Algeria, the FIS, and the experience of other Islamist parties and regimes in the region, some speculation is at least possible. This study offers a tentative map of the political terrain that lies in the future—subject to adjustment as more specific knowledge is gained about FIS operating characteristics.

First, on the international level, the FIS in power will probably demonstrate broad internal divisions—including how "international Islamic" as opposed to "national Islamic" its policy and ideological orientation should be. Initially the FIS will be overwhelmed by the magnitude of internal challenges and will probably not develop an immediate activist foreign policy. Over time, however, activism is likely to grow. Its key characteristics will probably include:

- Fierce independence; activism in Third World—but especially Muslim world affairs—on the bilateral level, international organization level (various Third World forums), and in the UN; for this purpose Algeria has a highly accomplished diplomatic corps.

- Assistance to other Islamist movements—not necessarily violent ones—in neighboring countries and the region; this does not necessarily mean a protracted effort to overthrow neighboring regimes, but these efforts will almost certainly be viewed by neighbors as threatening, partly in view of their own vulnerabilities.

- The sheer fact of the FIS gaining power in Algeria will have major psychological impact in the region by emboldening other Islamist movements, especially in Egypt, Tunisia, Libya, and Morocco—although the prospect of Islamist victories in those states will depend basically on the internal dynamics of each country rather than on Algeria's support. The FIS nonetheless can offer support to these movements in the form of asylum, financial aid, and even weapons—although most of the other Islamist movements have not been violent, except in Egypt.

- The FIS could easily be drawn into conflict with neighboring Morocco, with whom Algeria has had uneasy relations for decades. The two states are geopolitical rivals in the region, dispute borders (given by the French to Algeria), and have used the Saharan Liberation Front (or Polisario Front) in southeastern Morocco as a proxy of direct war. King Hassan of Morocco, on the other hand, has made a point of keeping good relations with the FIS.

- The FIS will likely refuse to normalize relations with Israel and will rhetorically denounce the peace process, but it will also be unlikely to significantly affect the peace process. An Islamist Algeria can, however, contribute to the maintenance of a generally negative attitude about the peace process still existing among some states of the Muslim world.

- The FIS will show a keen desire for higher gas and oil prices (a goal shared by most energy-producing states, but not easily accomplished); but economic goals, and not ideology per se, will influence the FIS's conduct of bilateral energy sales to the region.

- The FIS will probably demonstrate a strong interest in supporting Islamist movements in Africa south of the Sahara—possibly even as a potential rival to Iran.

- FIS will display a realism about dealing with the international economic order—despite discontent with it—and perhaps make some efforts to move it in more equitable directions over time. Algerian Islamist realism may contrast sharply with the Iranian lack of realism. Algeria is likely to accept and work with the international order, even while perhaps working to change it. It will not act as a "revolutionary" power toward the world as Iran has done.

- While FIS relations with the United States will of course be a two-way street, the FIS is *not* necessarily likely to seize upon the United States as the main source of Algerian problems or as the "Great Satan"—despite past FLN ideology in the 1960s and 1970s that often portrayed the United States as the center of imperialism. The United States actually has an unusual policy opportunity to defuse a major moment in the evolution of regional Islamist movements: It actually carries little historical baggage in Algeria, and the FIS considers it more "objective" than Europe about Islam, despite the strong pro-Israeli bent in U.S. policies. The FIS favors the teaching of English in Algeria as a culturally "neutral" language, as opposed to French. U.S. citizens, remarkably, so far have not been victims of violence—unlike other foreigners—by radical groups in Algeria.

- While U.S.-FIS relations should thus start out on a relatively neutral level, both sides are capable of allowing an escalation of tensions to occur through ideological overreaction to each other which, sufficiently mishandled, could result in the demonization of the United States.

- The FIS is likely to welcome U.S. private-sector investment in Algeria and to undertake close commercial relations with the United States.

- The FIS will be determined—as was the FLN—to make Algeria into a great regional power, including interest in the potential of developing nuclear weapons consonant with that status.

- The FIS has no tradition of international terrorist action abroad in general, but Algeria did use terrorism effectively against France during its long armed struggle for independence; terror has recently been exported to France, resulting in at least 17 different incidents as of November 1995, perpetrated by a radical armed movement.

- The FIS has long had good ties with Saudi Arabia and received a great deal of Saudi funding until recent years when the FIS adopted—somewhat belatedly—a pro-Saddam position in the Gulf War in keeping with the general mood of the population. A key ideological turning point will be whether or not FIS chooses to make Saudi Arabia an ideological enemy.

- Algeria as a state enjoyed good relations with the Islamic Republic of Iran until 1993, when relations were broken because of Iranian support for the FIS. The FIS in power will certainly seek to restore cordial relations with Iran, but it will emphatically not follow any Iranian lead; an Islamist Algeria indeed could ultimately become an Islamic rival to Iran in Africa over the longer run.

- The FIS has had good relations with Islamist Sudan as well and will work to maintain them; the FIS in power, however, might well ultimately find itself a rival with Sudan for power in Africa as well as for influence over Islamist movements there.

Domestically, the FIS in power will face serious problems in reversing a serious socioeconomic crisis of massive unemployment, debt, lack of housing, dwindling social services, and fraying urban life as well as a legacy of bitterness on all sides due to several years of brutal killings. Unfortunately, the FIS as of now has no clear-cut policies to address these urgent problems, other than to diversify the economy and seek investment; the FIS will be forced to improvise to a considerable extent and will be heavily dependent on drawing in educated bureaucratic and technical cadres to manage the state.

In the social arena, the FIS will almost surely seek to impose a level of Islamic austerity as a way of life—in dress (especially for women), ban of public sale of alcohol, and censorship of films and TV. It will not oppose women in the workplace but may strive to separate them there where readily feasible. It will probably adopt separate-sex educational institutions. There could be some nominal efforts initially to impose a few of the more draconian traditional Islamic punishments, but such punishments are not likely to dominate the penal structure for long—even Islamists disagree over this issue. All these austerities of lifestyle may be uncongenial to Westerners, and to many Algerians as well, but they are already familiar to many Westerners from Saudi Arabia, Pakistan, etc. Adoption of these practices should be of no strategic concern to the West unless gross violations of human rights should take place outside the context of austere Islamic law.

The FIS may actually have some positive contributions to make in the area of social programs. It has a close understanding of, and involvement in, coping with problems of the urban poor and is actively interested in the need to organize communal and neighborhood organizations, self-help movements, student and women's groups, sports facilities, better social services, etc. There will be immense pressure on the FIS to "deliver" in social terms, given the public disillusionment with the long failures of the FLN and subsequent junta rule. The FIS might also be able to substantially reduce corruption—at least for a while, and introduce other broader social reforms.

Impelled by a desire not to see the FIS/Islamist experiment fail, especially in the public eye, the FIS will likely be populist in orientation, thus requiring substantial income. The FIS will therefore be tempted to turn to some broader redistributive program to avoid social collapse. The FIS has no philosophical opposition to privatization per se, but many practical reasons, including long-term socialist precedents, issues of power, and control over the process of social change, will make it difficult for the regime to proceed with economic liberalization.[1] The need for revenue will probably inject realism into FIS international relations, more than is the case in Iran, or even Sudan. If the FIS comes to power via the ballot box, the pressures to produce at a visible public level will be even greater than power via a coup, as in Sudan.

IMPACT ON WESTERN INTERESTS

From a U.S. point of view, a FIS regime is not the most desirable government for Algeria, compared to a less ideological and more pragmatic coalition of parties—perhaps including the FIS. The FIS is untested and lacks a rigorously clear program, and its democratic intentions are open to debate. The FIS will not be as "convenient" to deal with as was the FLN or the current junta has been: it will harbor a general anti-Western suspicion and will likely present a number of regional problems. But the United States does not have much choice in the matter. The present situation under the current junta is unacceptable over the longer run and only polarizes the country more deeply. The junta, left to its own devices, is not likely to be able to rise to the occasion to rid itself of its authoritarian elements, although the November 1995 presidential elections (honest but unrep-

---

[1]A new Islamist regime in Sudan, under much less pressure, did in fact make serious efforts to follow IMF strictures for a year or more.

resentative) offer a small hope that President Liamin Zerwal may now feel he has greater strength to overcome the hard-liners within his own ranks. Just as possibly, however, and without major external pressure, Zerwal may continue to isolate legitimate political parties from rule, especially the FIS. Long-term nonconstitutional isolation of the FIS from the process will continue to destabilize the Algerian political system.

The West is thus almost certain to encounter the FIS as a major player in Algerian politics in some form. It might, furthermore, well be able to live with a FIS regime. The FIS is unlikely to present a massive challenge to U.S. and Western interests, even if it will prove prickly and difficult on the international scene; it could also prove ineffective in power and thus perhaps eventually gravitate toward authoritarian means as its policies over time suffer public rejection. It almost surely will not resemble Iran in psychological character or style. If the present Algerian spectacle of major civil strife and radicalization continues indefinitely, however, the more mainstream elements of the FIS movement are likely to become marginalized and the radicals empowered. Past Algerian government policies will then bear direct responsibility for the radicalization of the movement that was not so strongly present before, and in ways that now threaten the Algerian political scene for many years to come.

The problems of Western coexistence with ideological Islamist regimes will perhaps recur in several other Muslim countries as well, where Islamists gain a major voice in government or populations express long-pent-up grievances that include anger (both rational and irrational) at Western power, wealth, and dominance of the international order. While Western states would clearly prefer to deal with regimes that are pro-Western, old-style attempts by the West to determine the outcome of political processes in Third World states are clearly far less feasible today—or acceptable in the eyes of the world—and would tend only to delay the day of political reckoning. Change is simply long overdue in states like Algeria; when it comes, the process will, by definition, be somewhat destabilizing.

SCENARIOS BY WHICH THE FIS GAINS POWER

The question then is not so much whether the FIS will come to power, but *how*, and to what degree. Scenarios of FIS ascendancy to power via chaos, violence, government collapse, even social revolution, clearly present the worst possible political environment in which all political and social structures are destroyed, thereby facilitating the emergence of the most radical elements. Continuation of present hard-line policies by the Algerian regime in the end promises that very scenario—continued violence, turmoil, and the eventual collapse of a regime that cannot manage the crisis. But two other, more peaceful, alternatives exist for FIS accession to a major role in governance:

- First, a nondemocratic "deal" in which the military negotiates an agreement to share power with the FIS in a nondemocratic order; such an agreement perpetuates the absence of democratic governance in Algeria and simply delays the ultimate political show-down. But under these circumstances, the FIS would at least operate within a more controlled situation, developing its policies under some constraint, while gaining experience and hopefully wisdom about the exercise of power and administration. So far the FIS has rejected this "Sudanese solution" as a rejection of its call for democratic governance. Such a deal would also alienate the other major parties in Algeria who have supported the legalization of the FIS.

- A second, democratic, alternative would call for new elections in which the FIS might win a plurality to form a government, probably with other parties. This is perhaps the most desirable scenario for the longer-range development of Algerian politics, but could well be a messy sort of democratic coalition in the short term as all parties sought to learn, and work, the system. It would be the first time Islamists came to national power via the ballot box in the Middle East.

An electoral victory would place considerable psychological and moral strictures on the FIS not to "cancel democracy" thereafter, since it would be expected to depart office via the same means it took office; but obviously there could be absolutely no guarantees that this would take place. The FIS has nonetheless committed itself repeatedly to the democratic process, including the principle of "alternation" of parties in power, in joint statements made with the other major parties of Algeria. These commitments are hardly iron-clad—very few Middle Eastern ruling parties of any stripe have given up power willingly via the democratic process—but they provide the domestic and international order with some grounds for pressuring the regime, or declaring it illegitimate, should it fail to honor its obligations.

The FIS in power will probably fail to achieve success in many of Algeria's most pressing problems—given their magnitude and complexity and the FIS's political inexperience at the national level. The prospect of failure in subsequent elections could well impel the FIS to reconsider pledges to reconvene elections, pleading the need for more time to implement its program. But the FIS must ultimately be demystified and come to take its place as a "normal" political party in political process, bereft of any sense of "magic" that the Islamist program now has for much of the population. In the end, the FIS is unlikely to depart radically from the political culture of Algeria—a culture that has had very limited experience—but nonetheless a quite vital interval—with democratic practice.

U.S. POLICY IMPLICATIONS

The United States has quite limited influence in Algeria. Nonetheless, Washington is capable of helping forge a Western consensus about creating a process in Algeria that would restore the prospects for free elections and open a way to end the conflict. Priority must therefore go to the emergence of a political compromise that includes all parties that eschew violence. But several fundamental philosophical/political issues must be confronted:

- Is the United States willing to inaugurate democratic processes in which the Islamists stand a very good chance of gaining a significant voice in power?

- What steps can Washington take to create a broader European entente to coordinate an approach to the Algerian problem—particularly including France, Spain, Italy, and Portugal? France regards Algeria as its region of special influence, yet recognizes that its present policies are at an impasse and have now brought terror into Paris itself. Southern European states are interested in coordinating policies on this complex issue; most have relatively enlightened views of the problem and an awareness that a military solution can never bring a settlement.

- What steps can Western states take to encourage a democratic restoration in Algeria?   First, economic sticks could withhold further loans or loan rescheduling to Algeria until a political dialog is begun.   Economic incentives as well can be offered as political progress is made.   Failing that, the legitimacy of the regime can also be questioned until certain steps toward dialog take place.   The military can be offered selected carrots and sticks for returning to the barracks.

- The question of terror needs careful consideration: can the junta maintain violence against the FIS as a party with the aim of perpetuating a violent response—whereby the FIS thus becomes a "terrorist organization" and outside of any political compromise?

A European accord on a democratic resolution will give nearly all political parties, including the FIS, a great deal of what they want.   Such an accord might also lend a solemnity and an internationally monitored institutional character to that process that will make it harder, but certainly not impossible, for the FIS later to renege on prolongation of democracy in subsequent elections—even at the cost of losing such elections.   U.S. policy should also be marked by principle, i.e., above all the principle of establishing electoral procedures in Algeria—even at the risk that the FIS will win a major voice in government through that process.   A U.S. policy driven by the goal of preventing the FIS from gaining a major voice in government becomes simply a further perversion of democratic process, sending the wrong message to the region and delaying the hope of any normalization in Algerian politics or in Islamist parties.   The ascendance of FIS cannot likely be staved off; to try to do so will only increase violence and delay the process whereby political Islam loses its special status and falls into "normal political perspective" in the region.

ACKNOWLEDGMENTS

The author wishes to particularly thank John Entelis at Fordham University for his careful and thoughtful reading of the manuscript and his many comments on how it might be improved. The report is substantially better after including large numbers of his recommendations. I also thank Marcy Agmon at RAND for her reading of the manuscript and useful suggestions for clarity and issues for further treatment. I am grateful to the many Algerian officials, academics, journalists, and thinkers who generously made time for me in Algeria in offering their views of the country's political crisis and its roots. Thanks are also due to the author's many Algerian and Arab friends in the United States who assisted in offering ideas and thoughts. The conclusions, of course, are the sole responsibility of the author.

Thanks are also due to Jim Quinlivan, Mary Morris, and Tom Mc-Naugher at RAND, as well as to Jerry Green, for helping make the project possible; and special thanks to Rosalie Fonoroff and Shirley Lithgow for processing the manuscript.

Chapter One

INTRODUCTION

Algeria is in agony. One of the largest and most important states in the Arab world is in a state of virtual civil war. Over the past five years it has become the battleground of a massive ideological struggle involving a variety of conflicting visions and approaches to the country's future. It is fashionable, and perhaps reassuring to Westerners, to picture the scene in terms of modernism contesting with reactionary or medieval forces. This simplistic vision does not conform with a much more complicated reality made up of a variety of conflicting trends: democracy versus authoritarianism, a challenge to corrupted elitist rule, a search for cultural and political "authenticity," class struggle, generational differences, the imperialist legacy, and a huge debate over what it is to be "modern." Among the present regime and its Islamist opponents there are no obvious champions of a "right" cause with whom Westerners can identify. Violence should surely be condemned, but elements on both sides have been committed practitioners for many years now.

Even in the absence of appealing protagonists, the stakes are nonetheless high. A total victory by the radicals of either the military-dominated government or the Islamists will result in severe damage to the fabric of Algerian society. Failure to resolve the conflicts will lead to more instability and violence—and worse, to the growth of extremist goals, rhetoric, and means—that can only leave Algeria in paroxysm. Such an Algeria is a genuinely volatile presence for all its neighbors in the region—including West European states just a short hop across the Mediterranean. At its very worst, an Algeria under the most radical of the fundamentalists, while an unlikely scenario, could represent a new Iran—and it would be in a highly strategic location, owing to its huge gas holdings, its prominent position near the mouth of the Mediterranean, and its proximity to southern Europe.

In short, the stakes are high. The only solution to the problem lies not in the exclusion of the major cultural and political trends of Algeria—such a formula only guarantees virtually permanent civil conflict—but in the integration of its various forces. Yet while such a formula is easily espoused on paper, it is extremely difficult to accomplish in reality.

This study examines the nature of the fundamentalist, or Islamist, challenge in Algeria. It is a descriptive study, but one that is operationally and policy-oriented—it seeks to examine how and why things happen. The following key questions dominate:

- Why is the Islamist movement so powerful in Algeria?

- What are its strategy and main tactics in the political field?

- How might it come to power?

- What would be the consequences of its coming to power?

- What are the possible avenues of solution?

The first chapter of the study examines the country's political culture: What are the unique formative experiences that make Algeria? What kind of influence is this political culture likely to have on the evolution of Algeria's politics and particularly its Islamist parties in the future? The author devotes perhaps greater attention to the concept of political culture in the belief that this, however difficult it may be to define, is the critical variable in the behavior of states. Although issues of identity, legacy, ideology, and vision are extremely "soft" factors in analysis, they figure powerfully in the behavior of states and societies as the emotional engines of aspirations and actions. Individual political culture can be defined differently by different observers, and its degree of influence at any given time can never be predicted, but one ignores it at one's peril. Because this feature of politics is so often ignored, this study devotes considerable attention to it. If the author's vision of the political culture differs from others' views of that same culture, hopefully it will inspire countervisions.

Chapter Two examines the workings of the Islamist party, FIS: How did it come into being, what are its antecedents, and how did it benefit from the failures of the long authoritarian rule of the FLN?

Chapter Three examines how the FIS built power: What are the methods by which it has gained influence and power on the Algerian scene today? This process is one of the most important factors in understanding the character of modern Islamist movements. Do such movements come to power via revolution (as in Iran), by military coup (as in Sudan), or potentially via the ballot box, as may be the case in Algeria? What does the Algerian experience share, if anything, with Islamist movements in other Muslim countries?

Chapters Four and Five move into much more speculative areas of analysis in an attempt to outline what FIS policies might look like if the party were to come to power. Chapter Four discusses potential domestic policies, Chapter Five potential FIS foreign policies. Chapter Six examines an ultimate denouement of the struggle for power, how it might be resolved and the implications of various forms of resolution. This chapter, as well as Chapter Five, discusses U.S. interests and options in the situation.

Finally, the study notes points of comparison with other Islamist movements and regimes in the world. How and why do they resemble each other, and how do they differ? What does the Algerian experience tell us about the phenomenon of radical Islam elsewhere, and vice versa?

The basic conclusion of this study holds that the main Islamist party of Algeria, Islamic Salvation Front (Al-Jabha al-Islamiyya li'l-Inqadh in Arabic, commonly known as "the FIS," from the French acronym) represents a deeply integral part of Algerian society and draws upon powerful political tradition. At this stage in Algerian history, it will be very difficult, if not almost impossible, to stop Islamist forces from developing a major voice in power in Algeria. The question is only how and to what degree they will gain this voice. This question is all-important to the future of Algeria and its relations with the rest of the world. If protracted civil war characterizes the next few years of political struggle, the resulting legacy will be one of exceptional violence and bitterness on all sides. A FIS victory through insurrection, violence, and state collapse represents the worst possible conditions by which Islamists can come to power, for this would fuel the kinds of passions and excesses that marked the Iranian experience in 1979–1980. In such a climate all institutional restraints break down, creating the ideal environment for the most radical forces to pursue radical goals.

If the FIS came to power via legitimate means and due process, on the other hand, the constraints of constitutional procedure and other government institutions—presidency, army, parliament, economic institutions, and traditional social forces—would remain in place. This does not guarantee that the FIS would remain moderate in power, but it represents the optimum environment in which it might remain reasonably moderate, be under domestic and international pressure not to destroy those legal institutions by which it came to power and by which, presumably, it would eventually leave power. Under any circumstances, the performance of an Islamist regime in power may be trying both domestically and internationally—but there are only limited degrees to which it can be denied a major voice in power. To shut the FIS out of the political process indefinitely is only a recipe for increasing civil insurrection and guerrilla warfare as the country grows ever more polarized with no viable political alternatives on the horizon. Finally, Islamist governments in the Middle East are likely to multiply in the years ahead, taking numerous different forms. They, and the West, are going to have to learn to live with each other. The West's experience with the FIS therefore matters considerably.

THE LEGACY: ALGERIAN POLITICAL CULTURE

The political culture of Algeria and the nature of its historical experience are important to an understanding of the environment within which such bloody confrontations are transpiring. They offer, too, insights into some of the deeply imbedded trends in Algeria that are likely to emerge under almost any future regime. These elements of history are powerful cultural determinants that cannot readily be ignored or altered in the future evolution of politics there. While issues of identity, legacy, ideology, and vision are extremely "soft" factors in analysis, they resonate powerfully in the behavior of states and societies. Modern Algeria has its origins in an exceptionally violent anticolonial struggle and a dramatic role on the international stage. Yet, at least in the United States, Algeria is perhaps one of the least-known Arab states. What aspects of its distinctive history might offer insights into the character of its Islamic politics today?

THE INTENSITY OF THE COLONIAL EXPERIENCE

The intensity of the colonial experience is the single most important factor in the creation of Algerian political culture today. It penetrates and permeates the country's attitudes toward the rest of the world. The intensity has triple roots: first, French colonialism lasted longer there than it did in any other part of the Middle East—132 years.

Second, the colonial experience was deeper than that of most other Middle Eastern countries: Algeria was not just a foreign protectorate or mandate, as nearly all the other French- and British-ruled Arab states in the Middle East were; the French truly colonized Algeria. It was not merely occupied by foreign troops and administrators, but

5

was actively settled, as an integral part of France, by one million French citizens—colons—who lived permanently in Algeria, owned land, were represented in French parliament, and, in theory, would always remain there. The impact on Algerian life was sweeping.

Third, the struggle for liberation from colonialism was longer and bloodier than in any other Arab country by far. It took an eight-year war with perhaps as many as a million Algerians dead before the country won liberation from French control. Indeed, the loss of Algeria was a traumatic experience for France itself, almost producing a coup against the government by French right-wing military forces for whom departure from Algeria—"French soil"—was inconceivable. Numbers of departing French colons wreaked methodical and vindictive destruction upon facilities they had built: schools, hospitals, libraries, government buildings, machinery, etc.[1] The legacy of bitterness was long lasting—many French had lived as long as five generations in Algeria. The French are still reliving past Algerian traumas, as Algerian-inspired terrorism continues to strike Paris to this day.

But however traumatic the overall experience was for the French, it was vastly greater for the Algerians themselves, who paid a deep price in blood and struggle to gain their independence.

Finally, the Algerians suffered an immense sense of cultural loss. Whatever the virtues of colonialism may be in building an infrastructure, promoting economic development (usually highly skewed toward the particular needs of the metropole), and education, the cost to the national culture and psyche can be exceptionally high, forcing a people to depart from the path of "normal" organic self-development to one of external domination, subordination to foreign ruling cadres, and infliction of weakness, humiliation, and loss of identity upon the colonized. In the course of over a century of colonial rule, France banned all Islamic institutions that could serve to develop the Arabic language as a vehicle of culture: Qur'an schools, shari'a (Islamic law) courts, and the native administrative bureaucracy. Thus, "the Algerian was left without all supporting structure, unpro-

---

[1]John Ruedy, *Modern Algeria*, Bloomington: Indiana University Press, 1992, p. 186.

tected and despised by a European minority, an alien in his own land."[2]

The Algerian colonial experience was thus uniquely vivid within the Arab world. The drama of the struggle for liberation, and the national sagas and myths that emerged from it, have been the raw material of the Algerian self-image ever since independence. The very essence of modern Algerian culture is thus deeply embedded in the concept of conflict and struggle.[3]   And Algeria's impeccable Third World credentials were born of this same crucible. This quintessential "Third World outlook" has powerfully informed the Algerian image and is, I would argue, still a strong factor in the psychological makeup of the country, affecting all elements of the political spectrum—including the Islamists. The colonial experience thus lends to Algerian political culture today an intensity of outlook and approach, a powerful sense of determination, and a belief in the power of imposition of will to attain accomplishments of heroic proportions.[4] This factor thus probably inclines Algeria as a state and polity toward an activism—sometimes even tinged with a radical sense of mission—more perceptible than in many other states in the region.

ISLAM: INTEGRAL TO THE POLITICAL STRUGGLE

Islam, of course, has deep roots in Algeria. But this is not the kind of Islam long linked to state power as represented in the great Islamic cities of the Middle East such as Cairo, Damascus, and Baghdad; Algeria has never been a significant center of institutional Islam in its own right. Its Islam springs rather from Sufi and mystical traditions, from the *marabouts* or itinerant holy men, that have dominated much of North Africa's experience. Islam, as in so many other Muslim societies, was also the natural cultural rallying point of Algerian resistance to colonial control. Uprisings and resistance to French control regularly came from religious circles. An association of Is-

---

[2]Mourad Kusserov, "Islam in Algeria: Past—and Future?" *Swiss Review of World Affairs*, April 1994.

[3]Omar Carlier, "De l'islahisme a l'islamisme: la therapie politico-religieuse du FIS," *Cahiers d'etudes africaines*, No. 2, 1992, p. 196.

[4]Remy Leveau, *Le Sabre et Le Turban: L'avenir du Maghreb*, Paris: Editions Francois Bourin, 1993, pp. 128–129.

lamic scholars ('ulama) was founded in the 1930s to combat French colonialism; many of these Muslim leaders were an important part of the military anticolonial struggle, and even became a formal part of the Algerian National Liberation Front (FLN in French) in 1954.[5]

The postliberation Algerian state, despite its strong socialist orientation, explicitly recognized Islam in the constitution as a pillar of state and society. Islam therefore is not a stranger to the political order, although, as we shall see later, serious rifts emerged between Islamic movements and the state starting in the 1970s, leading to the sharp confrontation between the two forces today. Despite that confrontation, however, it is important to recognize that *the FLN and the FIS have a great deal in common*[6] in their national vision, as we shall explore later. Today, the FLN has significantly changed since losing power in the last decade; and as one of the two strongest political movements in the country along with the FIS, it shares the antipathy to the current ruling junta. But under any circumstances, Islam is destined to play a major role in the future governance of the Algerian state, at least for a period. The problem is how this eventuality will come about, and at what cost.

THE CREATION OF THE SOCIALIST STATE

The prolonged armed anticolonial struggle for national liberation was transformed after independence directly into a government of single-party rule typical of much of the rest of the postcolonial Third World and its socialist orientation. The state—especially the army—and the single party became almost indistinguishable.[7] The economy became one of the most statist in the Middle East, buttressed by socialist ideology and state control of most of its sectors. Algeria's strong statist tradition has been exceedingly difficult to break to date (reminiscent of East European problems of perestroika), and this almost surely will affect future Islamist policies as well, despite FIS claims to the contrary.

---

[5]Robert Mortimer, "Islam and Multiparty Politics in Algeria," *Middle East Journal*, Autumn 1991, p. 575.

[6]Carlier, p. 210.

[7]Cherif Belkacem, "Le FIS: algerien avant tout," *Jeune Afrique*, January 9, 1992, p. 21.

This statist legacy is strengthened by the "rentier" quality of the economy, i.e., the state's heavy dependence on "rents," or income from massive royalties from the energy sector. The "rentier state" differs dramatically from states financed by taxes levied upon the economic activities of its citizens, who eventually come to demand representation in government and thus a voice in the collection and disposition of their monies. A state that by itself produces nearly all of the national wealth finds its own power enhanced and, serving only a distributive function, is largely able to disregard the wishes of its citizens. Major energy revenues have in fact served to impede the process of political liberalization in Algeria, as they have done in so many other oil states.

THIRD WORLD ORIENTATION AND NONALIGNMENT

Algeria, by virtue of its long, bloody, and spectacular struggle for national liberation, had become a major cause célèbre in the non-aligned movement of the post–World War II era, gaining instant prominence upon its independence in 1962—one of the very last major world states to wrest independence from its colonial master. Algeria's first major postindependence leader, Ahmad Ben Bella, assumed a leading role among the leading nonaligned figures of the era: Nkrumah, Tito, Nasser, Sukarno, and Nehru. The nonaligned world outlook embodied a broad general suspicion of Western state dominance and intentions, marked by a bristling resistance to exercise of Western power in the Middle East and Third World generally. During their long and costly struggle against colonialism, Algerians were dismayed to see the major world powers either supporting France or standing equivocally on the sidelines until the eleventh hour. The experience left Algerian elites with an extremely negative view of the existing international system. In many arenas and in many parts of the world, Algerians sought to undermine that world order and to work for a level playing field in which North and South, developed and underdeveloped, would play the game of world politics according to new rules.[8]

---

[8]Ruedy, p. 211.

Algeria thus has long been a critic of Western political and economic policies, with an eye to the activities of Third World movements. Although growing pragmatism in the last decade and a half, along with the general fade of ideological strife in the world with the end of the Cold War, has brought a new moderation to Algerian policies, this intellectual legacy is likely to color Algerian rhetoric in the future.

ALGERIA AND THE ARAB WORLD

Algeria's long commitment to Third World politics and its shared Arab and Islamic nature naturally led it to early and strong support of the concept of Arab unity and particular support for the Palestinian cause, one of the preeminent Third World causes of the past decades. Algeria became an activist within the Arab League and a leading intermediary in the resolution of inter-Arab disputes. Indeed, it was only with the end of the colonial era after World War II that the Arab East (Mashreq) and Arab West (Maghreb) were able to come together as independent states to try to forge a new power bloc and regional vision.

Yet Algeria also retained an ambivalence toward the Arab world. One hundred and thirty years of colonial rule had substantially impressed French language and culture upon the Algerian elite—and a profound ambivalence of self-identification. Unlike the considerable ethnic and religious diversity of the eastern Arab world, the Maghreb is quite homogeneous in ethnicity and religion, with only one major ethnic minority—the Berbers. It is, therefore, more relaxed about its Arabness. Arab nationalism and Islam readily combine to the same ends, unlike in the Arab East, where Christian and Shi'ite differences compound difficulties of common religious and ethnic national unity.

And today's Algerian elite generally does not find its sole identification within the Arab world. Algerians will remind you that they are not part of the eastern Arab world. The Maghreb, after all, is also just across the Mediterranean from Europe, and has been in constant interchange with it since Greek and Roman days, as part of ancient Carthage. Algerian elites believe they partake of a common Mediterranean and even European culture to a considerable extent. Their novelists are influenced by European literature and often write in French. Where then, does Algeria belong?[9]

THE LANGUAGE STRUGGLE: ARABIC VERSUS FRENCH

Language is an issue of major cultural sensitivity in Algeria. In the colonial period, Arabic had largely been relegated to distinct local dialect, as the French suppressed its use for most purposes—most importantly in education. Thus, only a small circle of Muslim scholars maintained proficiency in the written language. After liberation, the damage done to the Arabic language in Algeria—a direct blow to the very soul of Algerian-Islamic culture—became a central cultural grievance. The regime therefore undertook a process of Arabization (*ta'rib*) of culture and education, starting in the 1960s, to restore the role of Arabic in educated circles, government, and society. The FLN expressed its principles in the following terms: "Islam is my religion, Arabic my language, and Algeria my fatherland."[10] New goals especially included the renewed use of Arabic in higher education. Language became the object of a government campaign; for a while the government even removed all street signs in French in favor of Arabic, at a time when only 60 percent of the population could read in Arabic.[11]

This portentous cultural decision had major consequences. First, large numbers of Arabs from the east were imported into Algerian schools and universities to teach Arabic language and culture. This act brought its own cultural content: a greater association with the rest of the Arab world in general, but particularly a broadened exposure to Islamist currents and trends of thinking from radical Islamist circles in Egypt, Syria, and elsewhere. Thus, powerful impetus was given to the development of Islamist circles within Algeria itself.[12]

---

[9]One Algerian intellectual commented to me that "Algeria has no friends in the world . . . except ironically maybe the U.S., in some strange way."

[10]Kusserov, p. 20.

[11]Rachid Tlemcani, "Chadli's Perestroika," *Middle East Report*, November–December 1992, p. 17.

[12]In this sense there can be no doubt about a broad process of "internationalization" of Islamic currents taking place throughout the Arab world over the past several decades.

Algerian religious activists thus became directly linked with such movements as the Muslim Brotherhood (al-Ikhwan al-Muslimin) in Egypt. As the FIS developed as a political movement in the next decade, it was to draw heavily on these contacts and influences.[13]

Second, the Arabization campaign opened up new cultural strains in the country as a fault line developed between French-speaking (francophone) and Arab-speaking (arabophone) communities. A whole new generation began to be educated in Arabic, giving it a cultural orientation different from that of the French-speaking class. But more than just a generation gap was involved in the trouble: elements of class and cultural discrimination began to creep in. Only some segments of the educational program received strong Arabic-language orientation; the prestigious and lucrative medical faculty, or technical schools, for example, remained francophone. Those who received education in the literary and law faculties were educated in Arabic and rapidly found that their swelling numbers made it difficult to get jobs, leading to an identification of their grievances with this cultural factor (Arabic versus French).[14] In fact, nearly all jobs in both the private and public sector require French, condemning those who lack that education to "dead-end jobs."[15]

As a result, the language question today has engaged the religious arena, since "the francophones" are now increasingly identified as part of the problem in what is also a war of culture. Yet the culture war is not rigorously synonymous with nationalism. Indeed, the earliest recruits into the Islamist movement were themselves francophone.[16] The army officer corps has traditionally been francophone, yet intensely nationalist. The francophone issue also takes on

---

[13]External Islamist influences, especially the Egyptian Muslim Brotherhood, also powerfully affected the Muslim Brotherhood in Sudan—which later became the nucleus of the National Islamist Front that was able to attain power by coup d'état in Sudan in 1989. While "foreign" or external influences can help inspire and shape Islamist movements in many countries, we are not basically witnessing here a process of "exporting the Islamic revolution." Domestic and local conditions are directly responsible for creating the critical groundwork of economic, social, and political grievances in which outside ideas do no more than help give shape to their articulation.

[14]See Francois Burgat, *The Islamic Movement in North Africa*, William McDowell (trans.), Center for Middle East Studies, The University of Texas at Austin, 1993, p. 257.

[15]Tlemcani, p. 17.

[16]Burgat, p. 257.

overtones of class and privilege—especially between those professionals with international connections and exposure and those who lack it—including many intellectuals. The francophones, by virtue of education and outlook, are hence more secular—another key fault line in the struggle between the current regime and the FIS. Islamists often refer to the francophone community—for all its diversity—as *hizb fransa,* or "the party of France."

In a fascinating twist, most Algerian Islamists are pushing hard for the use of English to replace French in Algerian education, and a small trend is under way. The Islamists say that English is "culturally neutral"—at least in the Algerian context—and more international, whereas French carries the colonial burden of the past and is laden with all the strong social overtones of modern Algerian society. English is also increasingly the language of science and technology, fields from which the ranks of Islamists are preponderantly drawn.

THE BERBERS AND POTENTIAL MINORITY PROBLEMS

The Berbers long predate the Arabs in Algeria: they even fought the Roman conquest. Great numbers were Christianized during the Roman period. The Berbers put up the "fiercest and longest-lived resistance to Arab conquest of any peoples met anywhere in the world," but then quickly converted to Islam once the resistance ended in the 6th century.[17] Berber was the dominant language of the Algerian countryside up to the 12th century. The Berbers today make up 20–25 percent of the population and are so identified by virtue of their native language, a Hamitic language related to Amharic, more distantly to Arabic. In fact, however, a majority of all Algerians are descended from Berbers, whose dominant blood mixed with a minority of Arab conquerors and immigrants; the vast majority of these groups, however, no longer speak Berber and have become fully Arabized.[18] The Berbers (a term from Greek and Latin historically related to the word for "barbarians") call themselves Imazighen and their language Tamazight, or Amazighi in Arabic. The main stronghold of Berber culture is Kabylia, the mountain region along the

---

[17]Ruedy, pp. 9–12.
[18]Ibid., p. 9.

northeast coast, but other Berbers speaking different dialects also live in the south, especially the Shawi and the Tawarig (Touareg), who are less urbanized and developed. Berber has not been used much as a written language, and Berbers are still debating over longer-term adoption of the Arabic versus the Latin alphabet. The government in recent years has permitted the use of Berber on the radio and on late-night television.

Whatever differences have existed between Berber and Arab in Algeria, the colonial experience tended to intensify it. French colonialists, similar to colonialists the world over, early seized on ethnic and cultural differences between Berbers and Arabs. The French romanticized past Berber Christian connections, felt an affinity to the mountain peoples and their culture, and undertook a major effort both to convert them to Christianity (basically unsuccessful) and to assimilate them. Some of the techniques they used were to build an unusually high proportion of French schools in Kabylia, provide special benefits and privileges, and encourage emigration to France.[19] The French devoted much attention to strengthening Berber awareness of their own culture, and academic research was devoted to Berber studies. In the event, efforts to evangelize the Berbers failed, and despite special privileges and considerable inroads of the French language, the Berbers did not prove willing to abandon their identification with Algeria or to support the goals of French colonization.[20] Indeed, the Berbers were active in the anti-French resistance later on, have made up a key element in the FLN, and are significantly represented even in the FIS.

Today the Berbers are known for great intensity of commitment to Islam, but they have retained a strong nationalist sensitivity about their own culture and have resisted Arabization, under all regimes. Indeed, they strongly reject the suggestion that Arabization has any part of being a Muslim. A so-called Berber crisis in 1948–1949

---

[19]Thus a disproportionately high number of Algerians living in France today are Berber, perhaps 60 percent, and their French language skills are highly developed all over Algeria. They are known in France to be hardworking; their remittances back home are important to the Kabylia. Unemployment among them in France has grown in recent years, however, opening them up to Islamist messages more than ever before.

[20]Ruedy, p. 99.

emerged when several key Berber leaders opposed the labeling of the nascent anti-French resistance movement as "Arab"; they insisted that it be called an "Algerian" resistance. Likewise, Berbers have expressed dissatisfaction even with many of the Islamic overtones of the nationalist movement, preferring instead a secular or even Marxist framework.[21] Indeed, the Berbers have shown a strong predisposition to the left, often typical of other minorities in other Muslim states, such as the Shi'a in Iraq or the Alevis in Turkey. Berbers today dominate the country's French-language newspapers, giving them a major voice in Algerian intellectual life, especially in secular circles.

While the Berbers are solidly Muslim, and have their own representation within the FIS, they continue to fear that Islamization equals Arabization, thereby threatening the independence of Berber culture. Berbers have consistently resented Arab attempts to rule Kabylia. In political terms, a key Algerian party founded in 1964, the FFS (Front des Forces Socialistes), has a clear and broad Algerian national agenda and vision, but because its leadership and main support comes from Kabylia, it has always been viewed (unfairly) as a "Berber party," harming its otherwise excellent electoral prospects among the population—much to the chagrin of its leadership.

Today, especially in an era of rising nationalism and separatism on a global level, the question of potential separatism in Algeria cannot be ignored. The very raising of the "Berber issue" by outsiders is seen by many Algerians as a "neocolonialist" effort to divide and weaken the Algerian state, as the French colonialists did. Algerians will tell you that they have no ethnic minority in Algeria, only a linguistic one. In one sense this is true, since nearly all Algerians have high proportions of Berber blood running through their veins. On the other hand, the Berbers of Kabylia have very much retained their own identity and language, even if that identity was lost centuries ago by much of the rest of the population so long Arabized. The Berber identity is strong and, under the intensification of global ethnicity in this post–Cold War era, is likely to grow, especially if challenged by the state.

---

[21]Ibid., p. 154.

With the intensification of the national crisis in Algeria, the Berber issue has taken on greater salience. A Berber Cultural Movement (BCM) has emerged that has called general strikes in Kabylia in a demand for a constitutional amendment for the acceptance of Tamazight as the second official language of the country. The state has been responsive to these demands, and has agreed to broader teaching of Tamazight, especially given the strong role of the Berbers in the anti-FIS movement; the BCM, however, rejects these concessions as insufficient. On the other hand, other Algerians, notably the secularist "Progressive Republican Party," criticizes these concessions by the government, stating that teaching Tamazight is "a waste of time and effort and a sowing of the seeds of division." It describes Tamazight as "a primitive language of no practical or scientific use"; it suggests the language issue was resolved "fourteen centuries ago" when Berbers accepted Arabic as their language.[22]

At present there is no serious likelihood of Berber separatism. But circumstances could change under a variety of negative scenarios for Algeria's future involving either strong Berber resistance to a future FIS role, or the adoption of harsh and divisive policies by the FIS, especially of intensive Arabization and Islamization in Kabylia, or French efforts to exploit differences within Algeria to weaken a FIS regime, or potential civil war within the country between the FIS and regional military warlords, etc. The Berber question therefore is an important factor in political calculations on the future course of Algeria.

SUSPICION OF THE WEST

The Algerian experience has produced an approach of overall suspicion toward general Western intentions and policies in the Third World and the Middle East—an attitude intensified by Algerian association with Arab nationalist movements in general, and close ties with the "socialist bloc" in the past. The country has therefore developed a somewhat prickly attitude toward Western power and goals as they affect Algeria and the Middle East. Such suspicion has permeated FLN foreign policy over the past 30 years and is even

---

[22]*Mideast Mirror,* October 10, 1994, pp. 13–14.

stronger in the army, which sees itself as the guardian of Algerian independence and the spirit of resistance to outside pressures.

Possession of major oil and gas resources can also help create paranoia among regime leaders generically, on two grounds. First, any state whose income depends primarily upon oil and gas is at the mercy of international price structures. The economies of the producers are thus vulnerable to these external forces. Second, energy is such a strategic international commodity that almost by definition, any major producer loses some element of de facto sovereignty because of the critical importance of that commodity to powerful states. Western nations historically have intervened in the Middle East many times, on both the political and military level, over "oil." Such precedents make producer states quite realistic about the international order, but they can also spark insecurity because of the high strategic stakes involved.

Almost any Algerian regime in the future is likely to reflect this tradition of suspicion toward the West, sometimes verging on xenophobia. What is unusual in the Algerian context is the addition of a certain pragmatism. Algeria has historically taken a cool and workmanlike approach to its dealings with Western powers, reflecting suspicion and distaste but also recognizing the necessity of dealing with them. Distance, aloofness, reserve, suspicion, caution, and some elements of rigidity, coupled with realism, are likely hallmarks of the political culture of this country for a long time to come under any regime.

THE ALGERIAN CRISIS OF IDENTITY

Algeria in one sense suffers from a far less distinct and historically rooted identity than its more self-confident neighbors Tunisia and Morocco.[23] The reasons are several. Tunisia and Morocco were long-time distinct historical entities—Tunisia the seat of the Phoenician-Carthaginian empire going back to Roman times, Morocco intimately linked with, and successor to, the flourishing civilization of the 800-year Muslim state in Spanish Andalusia until 1492. Algeria,

---

[23]Francois Soudan, "Les Islamistes peuvent-ils gagner?: Maghreb," *Jeune Afrique*, July 22, 1993, p. 13.

however, does not represent a distinct cultural-historical unit in the same sense. Indeed, it was France that gave distinct "national" boundaries to a modern state that had never been quite fully differentiated from the domains of other North African local rulers.

Second, as we have noted above, Algeria's colonial experience was far more harrowing than the much briefer and less actually "colonial" periods of Morocco and Tunisia. This experience more than anything else served to forge a new Algerian state, but its identity between French and Arab was painfully contested. Third, Algeria as a new state and a "new culture" was faced with the task of exploring its own national dimensions in the region after independence—a huge territorial presence with a new and uncertain regional role that had to be acquired. The crisis of identity will continue for some time, especially as the arabophone versus francophone fault line remains unresolved.

Indeed, many Algerian intellectuals will tell you that the identity problem runs deeper than just between the Arabic and French languages. Many Algerians, and not only educated ones, see Algeria as partaking in a multiplicity of cultures. They live far closer to Western Europe than the Middle East, and indeed do not consider themselves "Middle Easterners." Their economic ties are overwhelmingly with Europe, not the eastern Arab world. They are a Franco-Mediterranean people, an Arab people, a Berber people, a Muslim people. They touch black African civilization to the south. There are many competing identities here, then, that require working out. To highlight a sharp polarization between the Europe-oriented (francophone) and the Arab-oriented is in itself a considerable simplification of the issue, yet one in which France itself is deeply enlisted. Only when Algeria comes to terms with all these identities is some kind of resolution of national identity possible.

Unfortunately, that broader integration of cultures and identities is still some distance down the road. Today the Islamists are fighting exclusively for restoration of their Muslim heritage—at least that is the battle cry. The discourse of Islamic heritage versus the nationalist-socialist-secularist is a dialog of the deaf in which the two groups live apart in different rhetorical worlds.[24] Only mutual participation in the real world of politics will narrow the differences. While the political struggle may take the form of cultural symbols, it is issues such as economic conditions, employment, corruption, and the need for greater social justice and a more egalitarian society that lie at the heart of the problem.

*   *   *

All these features then, characterize the Algerian state after four years of bloody struggle that has not at all eliminated the possibility of Islamist forces taking a major role in government. It is these features of Algeria's historical, cultural, and political legacy that will impress themselves on any successor regime in the country, albeit in differing ways.

---

[24]Abdselam Maghraoui, "Algeria's Battle of Two Languages," *Middle East Report*, January–February 1995, p. 23.

Chapter Three

CONDITIONS FOR THE EMERGENCE OF ISLAMISM
IN ALGERIA: THE FAILURE OF THE FLN

Islamist movements have emerged in nearly every single country in the Middle East today. They differ broadly among each other, yet there seem to be some common characteristics as well. This chapter seeks to identify the Islamist phenomenon in Algeria, and to establish any common features it might have with the broader phenomenon internationally.

The FIS today is the dominant challenger in Algeria against the existing army-backed junta—the dregs of the former FLN regime. But the FIS is more a political movement than a mere political party; it is not even a coherent single political party at that, but a conglomerate of many different Islamic groups consolidated into one. It came into existence only in 1989 when the reform-FLN president, Chadli Ben Jadid, passed the first law permitting the existence of a multiparty system.

Of course, Islam is hardly a newcomer to the political scene. Clerics had long been active in the struggle against French colonialism. But the precise form of today's Islamic political activism has evolved over time, away from a reformist, society-oriented tradition and toward greater activism directly on the political scene. This transition reflects very significant changes in style that capture much of what the modern Islamist movement is all about. The FIS today is ultimately the product of this transition.

FROM REFORM TO POLITICAL ACTIVISM

By the 1930s, a strong reformist *(islah)* movement was under way, led by Islamic scholars. Its leader was Shaykh 'Abd-al-Hamid Bin Badis, the organizer of the Association of 'Ulama, which later became a component of the FLN during the armed struggle against the French. In the period preceding the armed struggle, however, the reformist movement set itself the goals of transforming and strengthening the social fiber and character of Algerian society in order to better resist colonial domination. The leading characteristics of the movement in the 1930s can be summarized as follows:

- The leading 'ulama were strongly influenced by intellectual trends in Cairo, Mecca and Medina, and Tunis.

- They focused on the building of mosques and the spread of popular literature and sermons on Islam.

- Propagation of education and culture were key goals. Youth were often sent abroad to other Arab countries for education.

- Vigorous campaigns were undertaken for the strengthening of Arabic-language study in schools and mosques, in place of dominant French in educational institutions. The central place of classical Arabic was stipulated by its role as the sacred language of the Qur'an.

- Leaders avoided activities that ran the risk of arrest. They opposed violence.

- Leaders were generally of patrician or elite classes, often distant and aloof from the masses. Their ethics and aesthetics usually reflected this upper-class background.

- They shared a distaste for Sufism (maraboutism), the populist, mystical tradition of Islam that is not under mosque direction and control.

- Religious schools and informal religious circles—not the mosque—were the venue of political activity, social life, and training.

- The movement usually avoided explicit fostering of xenophobia, harangue, or demagogy among the masses. Clerics sought to be models of excellence, to show Muslims how to do good, to promote justice and social peace, and to attain the enlightenment of the community.[1]

- An explicit struggle against French presence was not yet a central part of the agenda.

With the victory of the FLN over the French in 1962 and the foundation of an independent Algerian state, the role of religious groups changed sharply. The French occupier was gone, but the struggle for the character of the Algerian state and Algerian society was now at hand. As the FLN, now the ruling party of Algeria, began to undertake an increasingly socialist orientation, Islamist groups found themselves ever more uncomfortable with the secularist-socialist, even francophone character of the state and its ruling elite. By the 1980s, an astonishing transformation among religious groups had taken place: the main target of political Islam had now become the Algerian state itself—a state that had even formally embraced Islam at the outset as part of the national patrimony.

This type of transformation, in fact, marks nearly all Islamist movements in the Muslim world. The primary and immediate enemy is no longer the foreign oppressor (still an enemy, but more distant), but rather the state itself. It is the state that is now perceived as violating the Islamic patrimony and Islamic values and losing sight of the welfare of the community *(umma)*. At the same time, another decisive change has occurred in the traditional focus of the Islamic state: the struggle *(jihad)* is no longer for the propagation of the Islamic faith in *non-Muslim* regions, as it was throughout history; the real jihad becomes the propagation of "true Islam," genuinely implemented, within the existing Islamic community itself.[2] Finally, we see a move away from a social movement aimed at transforming public attitudes into a more Islamic direction over the longer run, to one that specifically aims at gaining political power in order to directly implement its ideological goals.

---

[1] For an excellent discussion of these groups, see Carlier, p. 214.

[2] Ali al-Kenz, *Algerian Reflections on Arab Crises*, Robert W. Stookey (trans.), Austin: University of Texas Press, 1991, pp. 111–112.

THE SOURCES OF ISLAMIST GRIEVANCE

The sources of public grievance are important for an understanding not only of Algeria's own political agony, but for much of the rest of the Middle East as well. The modern ills of Algeria reflect in part the broader crisis across the region. Algeria's situation is simply more intense and expressed in more dramatic and bloody fashion than in most other countries. Iran had preceded it, and Egypt, in many regards, may be following along much the same path.

The emergence of the Islamist movement in Algeria is largely a story of the disillusionment of the masses—and large numbers of intellectuals—with the long rule of the FLN. Ruling as a single party for nearly four decades with a monopoly on all political, economic, social, and cultural power, the FLN by the late 1970s was beginning to show serious failings.[3] The economy had prospered during the period of the oil boom in the early 1970s, when the rocketing price of oil and gas made huge new funds available to the Algerian regime. Much of these proceeds were used to finance costly imports of consumer goods that later had to be eliminated once the price of oil dropped at the end of the 1970s—creating serious social pressures.

Subsequent price drops have left the Algerian regime badly exposed, and in considerable financial debt—a challenge that has faced virtually all oil-producing states in the world. In effect, the FLN had ended up living off the "unearned" income of gas—leading to a distortion of the economy and a neglect of other productive sectors—a subtle trap for most oil- and gas-producing states. Consequently, Algeria under FLN rule today faces a growing crisis in food production: no longer able to feed itself, despite broad and rich agricultural lands, the state is required to import ever-increasing amounts of food which it then sells at subsidized prices, raising the foreign debt.

---

[3]For a scathing portrait of the corrupt, remote, imperial, paternalistic, and authoritarian character of the FLN in the eyes of the common people, see the portrait of FLN leaders as experienced in one village portrayed in a novel by Rachid Mimouni, *The Honor of the Tribe*, Joachim Neugroschel (trans.), New York: William Morrow and Company, 1989.

At the same time, an "increasing proportion of the population lives near the threshold of hunger."[4]

As with all socialist states, however, the centralized regime also impoverished the very soul of society itself. Popular religious expression, especially in the Sufi tradition, was discouraged by a puritan regime, leading to the blight of popular culture in general and its replacement by the official culture of the state. As one observer notes, "The politics of culture killed culture."[5] Public space in general disappeared under the regime, leaving frustrated and unemployed youth wandering the streets—the *hittistes* (wall-leaners), as they are referred to in Algeria—contributing to overall crime and social disorder.

The Algerian state also did little to foster the emergence of a genuine civil society—a characteristic failing of much of the Middle East—but the FLN's authoritarian single-party rule actively *hindered* the liberalization and pluralization of society. As we noted in Chapter One, control of oil proceeds by the state creates one of the primary hindrances against the development of any kind of liberalization: the regime is beholden to no one, and the citizenry must be grateful for any benefits of distributed state income.

A generation gap is also particularly vivid in Algeria today. The heroic sacrifices as celebrated in the epic of the War for Liberation have vanished as a living reality for ever-greater numbers of the youth of the state—where 60 percent of the people are under 25 years of age, and the birthrate is one of the highest in the world (3.07 in 1987).[6] The founding myths of the nation no longer speak to the youth, and especially cannot make up for failing economic conditions, massive unemployment—some 30 percent of the population may never have jobs—lack of housing, and social aimlessness. Unemployment for college graduates has been a particularly serious problem, especially when education in Arabic disqualified many for jobs that require bilingualism. Overall, the FLN has increasingly

---

[4]Will D. Swearingen, "Algeria's Food Security Crisis," *Middle East Report*, September–October 1990.

[5]Carlier, p. 189.

[6]Mortimer, p. 578.

been perceived as corrupt, insensitive to the needs of the masses, intent only on its own high style of life, and isolated from the people and their needs. Indeed, Algeria had never even been led by a civilian until the administration of the reformer Chadli Benjadid in the 1980s. To this day, the government remains under heavy military domination.

The FIS has thus moved—more effectively than any other group—into the spaces of discontent created by the failings of the FLN over the years. It is misleadingly tempting to think that Algeria's problems are primarily economic and hence can be resolved via economic means. This grasping at "rational" economic straws lies at the heart of the belief of the Algerian regime, and many of its Western supporters, that an improved economic situation will roll back the strength of Islamist movements. To be sure, a rising economy eases a great many problems in any society. But as we have seen, there are other factors at work here that help account for FIS success:

- There is a feeling of marginalization among large numbers of high school and college graduates who cannot find work "appropriate" to their officially educated status. Education, particularly in the Third World, usually marks a transition out of a class that survives by physical labor into one that becomes white collar. The resentment of this class helps fill antiregime ranks and creates an articulate opposition. While increased national income and a growing economy can create more jobs in general, it is at the level of white-collar work that much of the need arises. Expansion of the private sector would be a most important factor in working toward resolution of this problem. Class resentments are strong here, in a struggle of a nascent new elite against an old one.

- A process now under way of mass transition to urbanization creates deep dislocations. This problem is as much social as economic. With the familiar, comforting, structured social relations of rural life breaking up, urban life is dislocating to family structures, authority systems, community values, and the range of personal motivation. Urbanization and modernization, of course, is a universal phenomenon, nearly everywhere highly disruptive. While well known to the world, today the process is taking place at a faster pace and affecting greater numbers of individuals, who are more conscious of what is happening, more aware of the world around them, more politicized in terms of expectations, and more demanding than ever before. The regime cannot be blamed for the inevitability of the modernization process per se—although state socialism is not necessarily the most natural way by which this process can take place. When the regime seems to have mismanaged the process, it becomes even more volatile. In this sense, radical political Islam can be seen as growing out of the disorders of the development process. No other political movement seems quite as attuned to the full range of problems of urbanization as the Islamists, not just in economic and social terms, but even in cultural, psychological, and value terms.

- The inequities of the world order, in its distribution of power and wealth, are paraded in front of the world's population more vividly than ever before, thanks to global mass media. While inequities are as old as mankind, tolerance of them is shifting. Inequities are now increasingly coupled with issues of ethnicity, identity, and the demand for dignity and respect. The FIS has harnessed these impulses more effectively than other parties have done, although Arab nationalist movements, in the much less intense social conditions of several decades ago, also drew on these reservoirs. In today's Algeria, only the FIS effectively does so.

- The culture of the Muslim world naturally draws on the vocabulary of Islam to express concepts of right and wrong, justice, and equity. For large numbers of Algerians it *is* Islam that provides the first foundation of a moral critique of their own society. It is not surprising, then, that the leaders of the FIS and most of their followers would find it difficult to conceive of a moral critique of their society and government *outside* of the Islamic context. This reality strengthens the vehicle of Islam in politics and confronts the state with critics who speak in religion's moral terms. It will be difficult for other political movements to speak of these same social failures and evils effectively without recourse to the Islamist framework.

Islamist movements, therefore, are likely to provide the chief framework of opposition ideology and vocabulary for some time to come in Algeria and much of the rest of the Muslim world. But in the end it is *political* Islam, and not Islam the faith, that will eventually be judged for its "effectiveness" in meeting the broad spectrum of the population's needs. Only the failure of political Islam to deliver will eventually weaken its hold over the popular imagination. But such a test of Islamist efficacy can come only through the public's experience with political Islam in power—to one degree or another. Many educated elites and convinced secularists, to be sure, will hardly need to wait to witness the problems of political Islam in power to be convinced of its inefficiency. Indeed, Algeria's secular intellectuals and artists have been among the chief victims of Islamist terror.[7] But for much of the rest of the population, only experience with Islamism in power and subsequent disillusionment can bring political Islam down to the level of simply an "alternative political party" with its own predictable strengths and weaknesses—i.e., no longer "God's Party."

These issues, then, represent the major failings of the FLN regime that created an ultimately explosive political situation ripe for the Islamists to exploit. Many other Islamist movements in the Middle East have derived strength from these familiar patterns of failing state policies, corruption, lack of social services, inefficient state sectors of the economy, political repression, and lack of alternative political parties. Nearly all postrevolutionary Arab states suffer from similar problems of ineffective single-party rule in the name of the masses whose support is invoked in a project of nation-building. It was all these factors in Algeria that finally led to a massive public revolt in 1987 and the FLN's repudiation and effective fall from power, leading to intermittent reformist movements growing out of the old FLN—a liberal experiment that was finally terminated by the army takeover in January 1992 with the annulment of the parliamentary elections in which the FIS had won a plurality.

---

[7]See, for example, a discussion of the problem by leading Algerian writer Rashid Bujedra in "De-Konstruktion des Algerischen Kosmos: Der Schrifsteller Rachid Boujedra," *Neue Zuricher Zeitung,* January 7, 1994.

Chapter Four

HOW THE FIS BUILT POWER

How do modern Islamist movements come to power? This question lies at the center of the study of Islamism in the Middle East today. The quest for a means to power is naturally the central consideration of all Islamist parties—and indeed of all political parties in general. With only two Islamist regimes in power so far in the region today—Iran and Sudan—some initial precedents on the process of gaining power have been established, with possible relevance for Algeria. In Iran, the clergy came to power by a social revolution in which they had played only a part, but which they were also able to hijack and thereby ultimately assume total power. In Sudan, the National Islamic Front came to power in 1989 by a coup d'état, after many years of carefully building financial and educational strength for the movement and a following in the military. The FIS in Algeria now offers the first potential model of power achieved via the ballot box. But how did it attain a strong enough following to make such an event possible?

The FIS employed a broad variety of techniques to strengthen its movement, building toward its parliamentary election plurality (subsequently annulled) in 1991. These techniques include education, the use of money, propagation of a clear-cut message, modern media techniques, electioneering, use of municipal power bases and the ability to dispense largesse, and broad networks of sympathizers that reach into the ruling FLN itself. In most senses, these techniques are thoroughly modern, typical of successful emerging political parties in developing countries. Social mobilization, rather than underground organization, has characterized most of the FIS success—at least until the harsh state crackdown that has pushed the party into more clandestine forms of organization and activity.

EDUCATION

The effort to strengthen Islamist awareness and education goes back at least to the reform movement of the 1930s, when a far more conscious effort was made to inculcate Islamic teachings into the schools where possible. After liberation in 1962, the FLN firmly committed itself to the Arabization of education, importing teachers from around the Arab world to teach standard literary Arabic and to instill values of Arab nationalism in their students. (The spoken Algerian dialect differs notably from the Arabic of the eastern Arab world, especially in pronunciation; the state sought to make standard Arabic the norm and to establish literacy in modern written Arabic that is universal throughout the Arab world.) Many of these teachers were themselves Islamist and steeped in the traditions of the Muslim Brotherhood in Egypt.[1]

By 1980, Algerian Islamist activists, at that time referring to themselves as "Ikhwan" ("The Brothers," in reference to the Egyptian Muslim Brotherhood) had made a strong start in establishing a dominant position within many faculties of state universities. Campus gymnasiums and theaters were transformed into places of public prayer.[2] These activities were tacitly supported by the FLN itself, which saw them as a bulwark against the expansion of leftist influence on campus.[3] This time the leadership of the religious move-

---

[1] See Roger Kaplan, "The War for Algeria," *Freedom Review*, May–June 1994, p. 20.

[2] Rabia Bekkar, "The Shrinking Space of Algerian Politics," *Freedom Review*, Vol. 23, No. 3, 1994, p. 27.

[3] The use of the Islamists against left-wing forces was part of a global phenomenon in the 1970s and 1980s. The most prominent cases were in Egypt under Sadat, in Iran under the Shah, in Israel by Israeli governments anxious to weaken the power of the secular PLO, in Sudan under Numeiri, in Jordan under King Hussein, in Pakistan under Zia ul-Haqq, and in a large number of other countries. Such moves were tacitly encouraged by the United States as well, represented most boldly in the recruitment of Islamist fighters against the Soviet occupation of Afghanistan. Such opportunism, of course, has now come back to haunt nearly all regimes who today face powerful Islamist movements that monopolize political opposition, since there are no remaining significant alternative movements on the left to provide electoral competition. Algeria has in fact retained some alternative political parties, but as the

ment sprang not from the traditional clergy, but from lay activists who sought—in a movement reminiscent of Protestant teachings in the Reformation—direct access to the Qur'an and to emphasize individual understanding and interpretation of the texts in a modern political context, and to political ends. Students found themselves empowered ideologically by their newfound ability to read and interpret the Qur'an themselves and to challenge other authoritarian figures—including parents and even traditional 'ulama—on what the "true" Qur'an says and how it should be interpreted. The accent on youth strengthened the FIS immeasurably with new vitality, idealism, and activism—especially for those with almost no other alternatives.[4]

FINANCES

The financing of Islamist movements has been a significant part of their success. In Egypt and Sudan, large amounts of external money, especially from Saudi Arabia, contributed to the strength of these parties. Money has been regularly and broadly distributed by Saudi Arabia to Islamist movements worldwide for many decades, especially after 1980, in an effort to influence them and strengthen them against Iranian pretensions to the leadership of Islamism. It was not until the Gulf War in 1991—when so many Islamist organizations, ultimately including the FIS, turned on Saudi Arabia and protested the U.S. intervention against Saddam—that Riyadh began to reconsider these indiscriminate funding policies. Still, aid from wealthy private Saudi donors has continued, even after a change in official Saudi government policy closed off funding to radical Islamist groups—often groups that were outspokenly anti-Saudi. But the fact of Saudi funding had never caused many political ripples in Algeria, where strong long-term U.S. backing for Saudi Arabia would have made it difficult for the Algerian state to attribute subversive motives to these monies[5]—at least until 1990.

---

country moves toward greater extremism, the environment may squeeze out many other players.

[4]Carlier, p. 200.

[5]Belkacem, p. 21.

But foreign support should not be seen as the vital element in the political power of the Islamists. Typically, local benefactors, businessmen, and philanthropists contribute to the charitable activities of the Islamic movements. Various economic groups have seen an opportunity to build moral and social "capital" for themselves by contributing to the construction of new mosques in the Islamist cause. The building of mosques not only contributed to the well-being of many local builders and artisans, but also created bases for new "unofficial"—i.e., non-state licensed or controlled—Islamist clergy, who also showed their gratitude to their benefactors. Thus a range of people benefited: nouveau riche, as well as lower middle class, merchants, and small businesses, in the building of neighborhood political power.[6]

PROPAGANDA AND ELECTIONEERING

One of the innovations within the Islamist movement has been the politicization of the mosque. In most modern states of the Middle East, regimes have been careful to maintain firm control over the religious establishment, through ministries of religion, to include appointment of all preachers, and quite often, state determination of the content of Friday sermons—all to avoid a buildup of independent clerical power or criticism of the state from religious circles. Indeed, in Algeria a 1971 law permitted the state to control all mosque construction, and the content of sermons was centrally controlled. A generally "tamed" religious establishment followed state directions in most matters that could affect politics.

As the Islamist movement grew, however, it began to reclaim political control of the mosques. First, as we noted above, mosques began to be built outside the purview of state authorities, often funded by charitable private or external sources; as more mosques came available, they were able to serve as platforms for the FIS agenda. The regime could not always provide state-trained and state-appointed clerics to the new mosques built outside the state system and often, initially and reluctantly, allowed them to be filled by local candi-

---

[6]Carlier, p. 202.

dates, usually trained by the Islamists.[7] By 1989, however, in a spate of liberalization, the state had repealed laws stipulating state control of the mosques: the lid was off, and the FIS was to greatly multiply its ability to use the mosques as social centers, places for schooling and indoctrination, and as political centers. Neighborhood coffee shops were also taken over as political discussion centers for the FIS.[8] Not only did the number of mosques grow, but religious activists were able to insist on the creation of prayer rooms in factories, schools, and government offices. Loudspeakers were widely used to propagate the message, often in strident tones; cassettes of sermons by Islamist preachers in other states, especially Egypt, became widely available.[9] In effect, the FIS was actually engaged in creating a civil society to its own ends, quite independent of the state, and was able to penetrate the grass-roots life of the people in ways that the FLN had long since ceased to be able to do.

THE ISLAMIST PROFILE

In contrast to the profile of the Islamic reformers of the 1930s, the Islamists of the 1990s present a dramatic difference. Rather than elite in background, most of them are of modest origins, usually from the lower middle class. A technical rather than humanistic curriculum has usually dominated their education:

- Unlike the reformist clergy that stressed education, they tend to be poorly versed in the Qur'an and Islamic culture or theology in general. They have limited interest in the "texts" in general, and especially oppose monopolization of the interpretation of the texts by traditionalist clergy.[10] They speak rather of "jihad."

- They tend to oppose the traditional clergy, which is perceived as having sold out to the regime.

---

[7]Mortimer, p. 577. In Egypt as well, a similar phenomenon has taken place with the growth of unofficial mosques, usually under the control of Islamists and not the state.

[8]Bekkar, p. 28.

[9]Tlemcani, p. 17.

[10]See the very interesting generic discussion of this issue in Olivier Roy, *The Failure of Political Islam*, Carol Volk (trans.), Cambridge, MA: Harvard University Press, 1994, pp. 94–98.

- They are much younger than the older respected religious shaykhs among the reformers.

- Politics is their primary vehicle of action and accomplishment; activism thus ranks high in priority. They do not fear arrest, and are dedicated to a struggle specifically in the political arena. Unlike the reformists, they do not shrink from violence.

- They are firmly hostile to the entire concept of a secular state; Marxists are their greatest ideological opponents.

- They are interested in high-impact media and direct communication with the masses rather than in intellectual journals, articles, and intellectual circles.

- Rather than trying to raise the general educational level of the masses as the reformists did, they are interested in creating the largest political impact on the masses.

- The one unalterable goal for the Islamists is to come to power and assume control over the state, for all power is seen to spring from the state; the Islamist agenda cannot be fulfilled by means other than exercise of state power over the longer run. They are willing to reverse what they view as FLN distortion or abandonment of the Islamic heritage to which the FLN was in theory initially committed.[11]

THE FIS AND THE FLN

The future relationship of the FIS to the FLN will be one of the key determinants of future Algerian politics, since together they represent its two most powerful currents. Furthermore, despite their intense opposition to each other in the mid-1980s—the FIS as challenger to the then ruling and discredited FLN—there are many interesting points in common that might permit some cooperation in the future.

By 1984, the FIS had come to represent the primary challenger to the old FLN establishment. The FIS was a new force on the scene, owing its origins to the society from which it had emerged rather than to the

---

[11]Carlier, p. 214, sets forth this interesting profile of the modern Islamist activist.

ruling elite. It represented the grass roots of society—especially through the mosques—and the stirrings of a latent and potential civil society that had somehow survived the sterile years of official FLN political life.

In distinction to the FIS, the FLN in many respects had simply represented a political front designed to institutionalize army rule over many decades. The army set certain clear policy goals and limits, and then allowed the FLN to function as the sole ruling party within those limits—although considerable factionalism has of course always existed in the FLN ranks. As FLN's legitimacy collapsed in the mid-to-late 1980s under the weight of economic and social failure and broad public opposition, by 1989 the army itself withdrew its formal connection and support. The FLN during this time showed increasing divisions between a more liberalizing, reformist faction versus a conservative, hard-line antidemocratic faction.

Tensions within the army and the hard-line FLN grew as the key FLN liberalizer, President Chadli Ben Jadid, starting in 1988, opened the country up to an unprecedented and breathtaking period of liberalization and democratization in which he increasingly distanced himself from the FLN and its old guard. First, he perceived the need to bring about reform in the party itself, a process that threatened major vested interests. Second was the need to launch a process of "perestroika," of dismantling and privatizing much of the huge and inefficient state sector. Third was the need to open the system to alternative voices and even political parties. As of October 1988, then, after deep economic grievances sparked severe riots that rocked Algiers and were brutally put down by the army, Ben Jadid decided to permit the formation of political parties—even to include the FIS by the following year.

Over this brief period of democratic experiment (1988–1991), conservative elements within the army watched with increasing anxiety the weakening of the state's monopoly over power; they were finally galvanized into action with the major FIS electoral victories in municipal elections in 1990 and in the parliamentary elections of 1991. At that point the army took direct power in a coup in early 1992, without further democratic pretense.

Since the reform movement began within the FLN itself, that party has reflected a three-way internal divide: the old guard, the reformers, and the religious elements. The old guard has consistently resisted reform within the party and state (virtually synonymous) as threatening to privilege, entrenched bureaucracy and order—much as the old-guard communists have acted in the former Soviet Union. These forces lay behind the army takeover in January 1992. The reformers, on the other hand, still believe in the party but recognize the need to seek renewal of the FLN spirit as the guiding national ideology of the state and the population, as well as to reform a moribund economy and bring greater openness to the political process. While most of the reformers are strongly secular in outlook, and hence opposed to the FIS, their own critical views of the FLN have in practice served to strengthen the FIS assault against the FLN.

Finally, the FLN has always contained religious elements, particularly stemming from the inclusion in the 1930s of the Association of 'Ulama of Ben Badis into FLN ranks. These religiously inclined elements have long been uncomfortable with the FLN's strong secularizing current as well as with its corruption and inattention to burning social issues. This group within the FLN therefore sympathized with the FIS attack, and has moved closer to the FIS. They see it, in effect, as now attempting to accomplish much of what the FLN had traditionally tried to do in harnessing the population with the slogan *"fi sabil illah wa'l-watan"* (for the sake of God and Nation).

A key contention of this study, therefore, is that the FIS and the FLN are in some ways more similar in political philosophy than they are different; for many Algerians, the real issue is that the FLN became corrupted and ultimately misguided in its evolution, failing to attain the nationalist-religious goals it had set for itself. In this interpretation, the FIS seeks power from the old FLN (or the army) to do what the FLN could not do. Recognition of many of the philosophical points in common between the FIS and the FLN is extremely important to understanding the dynamics of Algerian politics today and the politics of the FIS tomorrow. In this view, the FIS represents the original and pure FLN vision, but this time adding the goal of an Islamic state to the agenda through application of the shari'a (Islamic law).[12] In the FIS view, in effect, "the political class has failed or betrayed the revolution; it must pay. Islam is retribution, but also the solution."[13]

Over the past four years, then, a regenerated FLN has come onto the scene as a "new" independent (and many-faceted) political party now ready to challenge army rule and to demand open elections. It has supported inclusion of the FIS in any political settlement to the current crisis. Earlier similarities between the FIS and FLN philosophies are now strengthened by their cooperation against the ruling junta. These events help us put the FIS in a more mainstream political context; in this light the FIS represents less of a radical break with Algerian culture or society than its opponents might like to claim. Some have jokingly referred to the FIS as the *fils* ("son" in French) of the FLN. Much—but not all—of the current political debate is thus really about who will implement the "Algerian agenda."

ISLAMIST AND STATE VIOLENCE

The FIS reversion to armed violence in January 1992 sprang directly from the army's coup, its annulment of the FIS national election victory of the previous month, its rejection of FIS activists who sought peaceful means to power, the subsequent arrest of hundreds of FIS leaders including its top leadership, and the outright banning of the party. These events changed almost overnight the character of the Algerian political struggle. What had been emerging as an uncomfortable accommodation between a reformist presidency and the FIS suddenly turned into a zero-sum game that has brought the country into a state of massive violence, paralysis, and guerrilla war. The army's act transformed the previous electoral struggle into a new military struggle that tipped the balance within the FIS in favor of its most radical and violent elements who had consistently maintained that democracy was not the path to victory. This radicalization of the conflict has further polarized the confrontation and rendered a compromise ever more difficult—not only between the ruling junta and the FIS, but also within FIS itself.

---

[12]See Lahouari Addi, "Islam politique et democratisation en Algerie," *Esprit,* August 1992, p. 146.

[13]Carlier, p. 203.

It would be inaccurate, however, to attribute the onset of Islamist violence solely to the banning of the FIS itself: a decade earlier a group of Islamic radicals headed by Mustafa Bouyali formed a group dedicated to the use of violence as a form of political struggle. Bouyali began a series of armed attacks against the state that lasted from 1982 until 1987, when he was killed by security forces. These operations left a legacy of violence that was inherited by radical elements within the FIS itself, and later led to the creation of several guerrilla organizations: the Armed Islamic Movement (MIA in French, or al-Haraka al-Islamiyya al-Musallaha), the Armed Islamic Group (GIA or al-Jama'a al-Islamiyya al-Musallaha), al-Takfir wa'l Hijra (Anathematization and Refuge), and other violent movements. These groups have been immeasurably strengthened by the shift of politics from the electoral arena to the arena of force.

Islamist groups dedicated to violence draw recruitment and support from at least four different sources. The first is the survivors of the Bouyali group, which included several new groups: the Association for the Struggle against Immorality, the Armed Islamic Movement (founded in July 1982 and active in guerrilla warfare and armed attacks against security forces in the mountains around Blida and Larba), and the Islamic Jihad, which was formed in 1986 by Bouyali and collapsed after his killing. Bouyali has become a symbol of bold armed attack against the state, and his name is regularly invoked by Ali Belhaj, the second in command in FIS. Two armed groups have appropriated his name for themselves, the MIA and Islamic Jihad.

A second source of recruitment to violent activism are the Algerian veterans of the Afghan war, or "the Afghans," who have come to play a prominent role in the struggle. Some 2,000 Algerians were recruited by the Saudi-based World Muslim League and transited Jeddah on their way to training camps in Sudan (years before Islamists came to power there) and in Pakistan before taking on Soviet occupation forces in Afghanistan. By 1992 most of them, battle skilled, had been repatriated to Algeria. They represent a particularly feared group because of their battlefield experience and effectiveness.[14]

---

[14]Marc Yared, "La deuxieme guerre d'Algerie a-t-elle commence?" *Jeune Afrique*, August 26, 1992, p. 43. These statistics are undoubtedly from Algerian intelligence sources and thus could be exaggerated or erroneous, intended to serve the political goals of the regime.

The presence of "the Afghans" in the fighting has led to charges by the Algerian government about the "international character" of the Islamic war under way in Algeria. It is important to note, however, that "the Afghans" are Algerian, and that they have not been recruited or trained originally for this combat at all. Clearly, they have received foreign training by Islamist groups, but this was for the Afghan cause—an "Islamic strategy" supported even by the United States itself in the struggle against the Soviet occupation of Afghanistan. While their guerrilla experience undoubtedly has lent radical Algerian Islamists much-needed expertise, they cannot really be regarded as evidence of external destabilization of Algeria, as the government often claims. Even more to the point, the conditions that led to the outbreak of discontent and subsequent major political violence are *all* domestically produced. In short, it is self-serving—and self-deceiving—of the Algerian regime to perceive its difficulties as stemming from external causes.

A third source of military expertise for the Islamists has been the volunteers from the Gulf War in Kuwait—on Saddam's side. At the urging of FIS number two, Ali Belhaj, dozens of recruits went off to Jordan for training in order to oppose the massive Western military attack upon Iraq. Their training was allegedly overseen by a pan-Islamist organization, the Army of the Prophet of God, in a camp at Kerak. Many of them have reportedly played a role in armed attacks and have threatened to kidnap foreigners in Algeria who support the Algerian regime.[15]

A final source of conscripts for the radical Islamists comprises deserters from the Algerian army.[16] As the army's struggle against the Islamists has grown more violent, the number of defectors has increased over the years, sometimes including whole units. Weapons have reached the Islamists from military supplies, seized in raids that often appear to have been facilitated by "insiders" within the military camps.

In fact, the Algerian military contains most of the same divisions that exist within Algerian society or the FIS. Although hard information is

---

[15]Yared (1992), p. 44. This information too, is most likely from Algerian government sources and possibly self-serving.

[16]Ibid., p. 44.

extremely difficult to come by, there are broad elements of sympathy and support for the FIS within the military ranks at all levels, even if such support is not fully revealed right now. Anecdotal evidence suggests this, as well as the experience of the military in Egypt, Sudan, and Iran in years past. If the balance of power should shift more sharply against the state, FIS sympathizers in the army could declare themselves. They are probably least numerous in the top ranks of the military, where political credentials are most essential to high office. Such reservoirs of sympathy with the FIS could represent an important element in the political equation in the years ahead.

One veteran observer of the Algerian scene, Hugh Roberts, believes that the MIA has never actually sought to come to power by revolution, but is using its armed attacks against the state to demonstrate the power of the Islamists and the need for the state to come to terms with it. Thus, the MIA "has never attempted to mobilize popular support on a large scale or to provoke a collapse of the state by targeting senior power holders." In line with this view, the MIA would thus be willing to come to terms with the state in a true dialog.[17] Debate has ensued among FIS members as to whether the organization should be associated with the armed struggle at all, if it is to retain its credibility as a political force—especially when French and U.S. policies have emphasized the need for junta dialog "with all political groups that eschew violence."

According to this same analysis, the truly dangerous force among the Islamic armed radicals comprises the Armed Islamic Group (GIA), which grew out of the Bouyali group, and the "Afghans," whose numerous elements had never been part of the FIS and were opposed to its constitutional strategy. The GIA has been responsible for great amounts of violence, in particular its death threats against all foreigners working in Algeria—resulting in a total of 48 foreign dead from September 1993 to July 1994. Thus, "the GIA has been a massive embarrassment for the FIS and the MIA." It has in effect challenged the MIA to competition, increased the army's hard-line op-

---

[17]Hugh Roberts, "Algeria Between Eradicators and Conciliators," *Middle East Report*, July–August 1994, pp. 24–25.

position to dialog with *all* Islamic groups, and forced the FIS to resist negotiations as well.[18]

Radical support to the FIS itself (excluding the non-FIS GIA) thus comes from a broad spectrum, stemming from three main organizations—the MIA, Al-Takfir wa'l Hijra, and Al-Jihad—as well as many smaller groups. The MIA, the preeminent organization, operates in all parts of Algeria. Takfir is related, at least in ideological terms, to the organization of the same name founded in Egypt in 1971; *takfir* means to anathematize, to declare Algerian society to be "impious" and profane, and thus to justify undertaking armed struggle against the entire state structure and its representatives. It controls several mosques in Algiers. Al-Jihad '54 is the armed wing of the Faithful to the Oath, and in 1992 it published a list of 1,000 targets for assassination, mostly consisting of police, military officers, and judges. Two other organizations declare loyalty to the Khomeini line of Iran: The Phalange of Jerusalem (Kata'ib al-Quds) and The Sunna and the Shari'a; they are both Shi'ite, although Algeria has virtually no Shi'ite population. Finally there is Hizbollah, founded in 1990, which is the armed wing of an esoteric organization founded in Pakistan whose Islamic beliefs are totally nonorthodox (and would be rejected by nearly all mainstream Islamists) but who engage in violent acts. All of these smaller organizations distinguish themselves more by their communiqués than by their actions.[19] But their diversity suggests two things: the intensity and range of the struggle, and the elements that will ultimately need to be brought to heel by *any* future Algerian government, including an Islamic one.

The FIS itself has never claimed responsibility for any acts of violence. Indeed, many Algerian observers doubt that the imprisoned top leadership of the FIS is able to influence the campaign of violence under way today anyway, especially by the GIA.[20] But do they actually want to stop it? In the face of state violence against the FIS— starting with the annulment of the legitimate elections of 1990, the

---

[18]Ibid., p. 25.

[19]Yared (1992), p. 45. As noted above, most of this detailed information dates from 1992; some organizational changes since then are reflected in the text, others are not.

[20]Jonathan C. Randal, "Islamic Front Steps up Struggle in Algeria," *Washington Post,* June 6, 1994.

banning of the party, declaration of a state of emergency, expulsion of FIS preachers from their mosques, replacement of 845 legitimately elected FIS municipal mayors from their posts, the arrest of party leaders, dissolution of the party and confiscation of its properties, the banning of its newspapers, the internment of now up to at least 30,000 activists—the party not surprisingly believes that war has been declared against it; it is thus inclined to react in harsher and more threatening tones. FIS co-leader 'Ali Belhaj has again spoken of "the right of Muslims to take up arms against an impious state."[21] Other observers suggest that the FIS objectively supports acts of violence because of their polarizing effect on the internal situation; they also suggest that the regime itself is taking advantage of the violent environment to settle its old scores[22]—such as the assassination of Prime Minister Muhammad Boudiaf, who had pursued corruption within FLN ranks too vigorously.

Whatever groups conduct the violence, there is a ready reservoir of disillusioned youth to turn to it. The strength of the armed resistance comes not only from the organizational skills of individual groups, but from the style of guerrilla warfare. In one sense, this mass participation cannot even be called true guerrilla warfare, since urban operations require no bases, no uniforms, no logistical supply lines and support, no flow of modern arms. Individuals have little meaningful organizational information to betray to the authorities. They live at home and are fed by their families. As anonymous individuals they live in greater safety than their uniformed targets in the cities.[23]

Even if the FIS claims no acts of violence for itself, as a movement it has always been an umbrella organization in addition to its role as a party, and has included groups that are active in violence in one capacity or another. It may well be that the top leadership of the movement does not itself advocate violence, but their goals are nonetheless served by those who do in the name of the Islamic cause. Could the FIS stop most of the violence emanating from the Islamist side? It says it cannot. In reality the real question is, What

---

[21]Yared (1992), p. 46.

[22]Kaplan, p. 20.

[23]Najib Mileb, "Algerie: l'impossible victoire de l'armee," *Jeune Afrique*, July 22, 1993, pp. 14–15.

price would the FIS be willing to pay to end Islamist violence? It is not likely to be willing to expend the necessary moral and physical force to do so unless there are extremely concrete gains to be had from the effort, such as a clear-cut opportunity to come to power.[24]

It is difficult, then, to say that the FIS is nonviolent. The more appropriate question is this: Is the FIS willing to come to terms with the regime, or does it seek absolute victory? Would it have the ability to speak for the majority of Algerian Islamists in reaching a settlement with the government? And most crucially, would it have the ability to bring Islamist violence to heel in Algeria after coming to some kind of position of power—especially such groups as the GIA that are outside the purview of the FIS at the present time? FIS tolerance of a considerable variety of groups within its broad ranks, including those dedicated to armed violence, reflects in part the overall atmosphere of violence that pervades Algerian politics today. But that tolerance too, theoretically could be withdrawn if political circumstances merit it.

How would the FIS then actually fare in such a showdown within Islamist ranks? The dynamic of the situation suggests that it could exert considerable muscle, especially if the stakes were high. It has shown impressive drawing power within the country. It is hard to imagine another party able to perpetuate armed violence for long if the FIS attains a large part of its political agenda and assures its followers of that fact. But in reality the situation is not likely to emerge with a clear FIS victory or full FIS control of the instruments required to suppress fringe radical Islamist groups. A FIS victory—either by ballot or by seizure of power in an Iranian-style breakdown of authority—could well be challenged by isolated elements of the military, leading to continuing violent struggle in which the FIS could not control all elements of the situation, including its own radical elements.

---

[24]This situation bears some parallel to the situation between Hamas and the PLO in the West Bank, where Arafat is willing to reach political accommodation with Israel but pays a high price among his own population in seeking to quell the violent activities of Hamas. Yet who in the end is most capable of suppressing Hamas violence, Israel or the Palestinian mainstream?

THE FIS AND THE GUERRILLA STRUGGLE

The FIS is engaged in a major internal debate over the relationship of the party to the armed struggle. The debate contains at least two major schools of thought. The first is held by the so-called parliamentary group of the FIS—individuals elected to the parliament in the 1991 elections. This group perceives the armed struggle as essential at this point in order to force the regime to return to the status quo ante and to hold elections as it was committed to do before the January 1992 coup. This group insists that all armed groups stay outside of FIS, and, in effect, outside of FIS control for the time being, since the FIS does not want to compromise its *political* position by participating in an armed struggle or "terrorism." At the same time it seeks the unification of all armed groups, both to strengthen their clout and, more important, to make it possible to rein them in once the political goals of the FIS have been met. The FIS does not want uncontrolled minigroups of guerrillas, each with its own political agenda, operating after the FIS has reached political agreement, a state of affairs that could result in further civil war between fringe elements of the military right wing and Islamist extremists.[25]

An alternative view within the FIS has sought to disassociate the FIS from all violence and armed struggle altogether. It seeks to bring the so-called MIA under firm FIS control as a guerrilla organization and to end its terrorist activities—although the line between "terrorism" and guerrilla struggle is highly blurred. The relationship between the FIS and the MIA has also been much debated. The parliamentary group insists it is not part of the FIS—which is defined by the FIS executive committee—because of the need to keep the FIS as a political party separate from armed guerrilla movements. The MIA (also known as the AIS) in fact is a force in only two or three *wilayas* (provinces), compared to the massive GIA presence in the country.[26]

---

[25]The FIS had initially encouraged the growth of regional minigroups of *mujahidin* (Islamist fighters) in 1992, since they were much harder for the state to penetrate than a single organization. The parliamentary group of the FIS changed its policy on May 13, 1994 to support unification of all fighters *outside* of the FIS.

[26]Most of the material in this subsection is drawn from interviews in November 1995 with Anwar Haddam, the FIS (and parliamentary delegation) representative in Washington, D.C.

A third Islamist view, basically outside of the FIS, is maintained by the GIA, which is committed to the violent overthrow of the state. The GIA has been the most violent of all Islamist groups in Algeria and has struck against a broad range of targets, not just government officials but foreigners, artists, journalists, and writers. The GIA, more than any other Islamist group, has created a sharp backlash against the broader Islamist movement because of its high degree of bloody-mindedness and ideological fanaticism. The GIA rejects any negotiation with the junta and reaffirms the "group's complete opposition to any reconciliation, any truce, any dialogue with renegade governments."[27]

The GIA does indeed challenge FIS leadership. It its view, the FIS no longer exists as a party, since it has been banned and represents a disparate group of Islamist activists. The GIA anticipates a long guerrilla struggle against the ruling junta in which the FIS has no appropriate role, and thus it believes the FIS should be dissolved. The FIS itself, of course, is extremely focused on preservation of itself as a party and as the preeminent political Islamist force in the country. The GIA and FIS can thus be seen in three different lights: (1) as rivals for leadership of the same political movement, (2) as proponents of differing strategies on how to come to power (armed struggle versus political activism), and (3) as differing elements of a phased approach to eventual political victory against an intransigent state (first armed struggle, then political negotiation). There are elements of truth to all three aspects, but it would seem virtually certain that a strong political rivalry will survive, even into a political phase of negotiation with the regime. At that point, the issue emerges as to how to bring armed groups to heel, and the degree to which they will be subordinate to an external political leadership. It is one of the tragedies of the Algerian agony that the state has critically strengthened the force of the guerrilla groups—a problem that will eventually afflict *all* of the country's political elements.

---

[27]John C. Entelis, "Political Islam in Algeria: The Non-violent Dimension," *Current History*, January 1995, p. 17.

THE EXPORT OF VIOLENCE

The Algerian conflict entered an important new phase in 1994–1995 as the armed struggle "emigrated" to France, including eight bombing incidents on Paris streets and subways that killed seven people and wounded 170, and a spectacular Air France plane hijacking that briefly raised the prospect of a full airliner being deliberately crashed into downtown Paris. The onset of terrorist operations that have cost the lives of over a dozen people, mostly French citizens, primarily reflects a determination of radical Algerian groups to warn French policy away from full economic and political support for the junta in Algeria—including support for the deeply flawed "presidential election" of November 1995 in which none of the major Algerian political parties were represented.

At the same time, some suspicion had arisen, including among French analysts, that the Algerian intelligence services had infiltrated and were manipulating several Algerian terrorist groups both to sow disinformation and support terrorist acts in a desire to bring the West—especially France—around to the conviction that the Islamists represented an unacceptably violent movement. Such tactics are of course well known in the annals of many intelligence services that have pinned acts of violence on opposition political groups in order to discredit them. In several cases, the GIA and the FIS have explicitly disavowed certain acts, including the distribution of bulletins in the name of the GIA threatening violence against foreign embassies in Europe.[28]

Fears about the importation of Algerian political violence to France are of course central to French policies designed to support the present Algerian regime, even though Paris has repeatedly called for a political dialog among the parties who reject violence in Algeria as the only way to reach eventual settlement. Given the presence of nearly one million Algerians in France itself, it seems hard to imagine that violent political conflict in Algeria will not find some kind of reflection on a regular basis on French soil as well; the degree to which Paris plays a controversial role in an Algerian civil struggle will also inevitably involve France itself in the struggle. Terrorism regrettably

---

[28]See the discussions of this issue in *Mideast Mirror,* October 19, 1995, p. 10; October 18, 1995, p. 17; October 16, 1995, p. 18; January 31, 1995, p. 19; January 5, 1995, p. 21.

"works": terrorist incidents in Paris directly enlist the attention of all French citizens and other political parties in the debate over Algerian policy.

The state's own use of extreme violence—characteristic of the Algerian state in the past several years—is of course a chief source of Islamist violence as well; hard-liners in the junta probably deliberately seek to paint the entire FIS as "terrorist" and hence permanently unfit for inclusion in any negotiations.

Three critical issues require resolution before any cessation of violence is conceivable on the Algerian political scene:

- The FIS will have to be included in any political dialog with the state before it will ever authorize any kind of end to political violence.

- The regime will have to end its extreme violence against Islamist groups before any agreement can be reached with the FIS about cessation of Islamist violence, i.e., it is not a one-way street.

- The FIS will have to develop the necessary political control over Algerian guerrilla groups in the event of motion toward a genuine political settlement. Violent rejectionist fringe groups will always exist, but they can eventually be marginalized in the event of general political progress, as the Palestinian case is gradually demonstrating.

Chapter Five

HYPOTHESES ON THE FIS IN POWER: DOMESTIC POLICIES

What would the FIS do if it came to power? Speculation about such an event ranges from the horrified to the resigned. The simple answer is that no one knows what the FIS will do in power—probably not even the FIS itself. Most of the answer depends on many variables: which specific personalities come to power, how, when, and under what circumstances and constraints. But such an event is too critically important, too likely to become a reality, to be simply dismissed as unknowable. This study posits that the FIS will almost surely come to power eventually, either in some kind of power-sharing arrangement or in full control of the regime. The analyst must therefore at least offer a range of considered speculation and his rationale for those speculations, inviting others to amend them as they see fit. For the purposes of the present analysis, we will consider what FIS policies might look like if the party came to absolute power, i.e., no power-sharing arrangement, but not by violence, military victory, or revolution, rather by election or extraconstitutional arrangement.

Islamists out of power the world over are notoriously vague when it comes to discussing concrete policies and programs, and the FIS is no exception. Islamists first retreat to the slogan *Al-Islam huwwa al-hall*—"Islam is the solution." Yet of course Islam has very little to say about the kinds of contemporary problems faced by most Muslim societies, except by way of generalized approach or philosophical and ethical foundations. The second broad generalization of the Islamists is that application of the Shari'a, or Islamic law, will indicate the directions of the solution. Yet again, the Shari'a has very little to say about the workings of modern societies in specific terms—so little that there is no Muslim country, including Saudi Arabia and Iran, that has not embraced a substantial body of non-Islamic law to supplement the broad application of the Shari'a where feasible; indeed, there are many cases of the nonapplication of existing Shari'a law.

Several sources exist from which we can derive at least some sense of what FIS policies might be.

- The actions and behavior of the FIS in power in various municipalities around Algeria;

- Indicators possibly gleaned from the policies of Islamist regimes in power in other states;

- Speculation about what we might logically expect under various circumstances of FIS accession to power in Algeria, based on the suppositions above as well as a general sense of Algerian political culture.

POLICY POSITIONS TAKEN

First, there is no unanimity among Islamist groups in Algeria, or in any other country, except perhaps on the most basic of issues such as the role of Shari'a law. (Even here the eventual timing and character of implementation of the Shari'a is seen differently, some perceiving it as quickly implementable into the legal system, others viewing it as an ideal legal state attainable only after the profound Islamization of society itself.) Differing policy positions have been taken by different Islamist groups under varying circumstances—usually by groups out of power—so that many policy positions may be tactical or opportunistic. Nonetheless it is instructive to note some of their political stances.

The FIS, being a grouping of various Islamist tendencies, not surprisingly has internal divisions. The most basic division is between the "internationalists" and the "Algerianists." The internationalists represent the more radical and theoretical elements who are less interested in legal sovereignty among Muslim states but prefer to think in terms of the world Islamic community *(umma)* as a whole. The Algerianists, on the other hand, focus primarily on the interests of Algeria and the Algerian Islamist movement, with less regard for international Islamic politics. Predictably, the internationalists are less hindered by the immediate realities and can take more abstract, radical positions, with less concern for the immediate consequences for Algeria at any one time. The Algerianists are more practical and pragmatic, some might even say opportunistic, in judging how an issue will help or hinder the party in its search for attaining power.[1] An alternative way of viewing divisions within the FIS is whether power should spring from the bottom up—characterizing the policies of 'Abbasi Madani, Rabih Kabir, Anwar Haddam, and 'Abd-al-Qadir Hashani—or be imposed from the top down—more typical of 'Abd-al-Qadir Shabuti, Sa'id Makhlufi, and others.[2]

POWER

Accession to power is a single-minded focus of most elements of the Islamist movement. The FIS believes that in a contest with state power, the state holds all the cards. The Islamists therefore seek power to enable them to break the state's hold on society and to have the means to create a new society. This does not automatically imply total opportunism, since the FIS claims it will not strike a "Sudan-type deal" with the regime, that is, agree to accept a nonconstitutional arrangement of power sharing with the army. Nor does FIS opportunism suggest that Islamists would of necessity use absolute power to impose their views against all resistance—à la Bolshevism. But it is a revolutionary rather than evolutionary philosophy in the sense that the first focus is the achievement of power with which to bring about change, rather than seeking the transformation of society through propagation *(tabligh)* of the true word of Islam, the goal of reformers in past decades. This kind of constant tradeoff between principle and expediency is hardly unique to the Islamists but is well known to all political parties, including democratic ones. It is mis-

---

[1]These differences very roughly correspond to the ideological debate between Trotsky and Stalin in the Soviet Union in the 1920s, when Trotsky called for support of the international communist movement as the first priority of the Soviet state, whereas Stalin called for "socialism in one country." These debates are still reflected in Iran as well, where clerical radicals are concerned with the Islamic ideological purity of Iran's position on international Islamic issues with less regard for their practical impact on their nation's interests or on its general international isolation; these positions contrast with President Rafsanjani and other pragmatists much more concerned with how Iran's foreign policies affect its domestic welfare.

[2]I am indebted to John Entelis for this observation.

leading, therefore, to state that "the FIS is only interested in power" any more than the ruling junta is.

DEMOCRATIC GOVERNANCE

No observer of Algeria can satisfactorily resolve the question about the FIS's ultimate commitment to democratic procedure. The FIS is not sufficiently transparent in its inner workings, it contains too many conflicting views, and in the end, circumstances will go a long way in dictating how democratic the FIS in power may be. It is probably not realistic to expect the FIS to uphold and sustain the democratic process, since no other party or group in Algeria (or most other Arab countries) has yet been able to meet such a standard. The raw reality is that democracy has scarcely been part of the Algerian experience, except for the very exhilarating and vital period between 1988 and 1991. Algeria, and even the FIS, may yet surprise foreign observers, but the fact is that its democratic experience is extremely limited and hence one must be extremely cautious about any future Algerian government's willingness to step down after losing an election.

There is a broad range of opinion about the FIS approach to democracy, ranging from the belief that it has developed some appreciation for numerous democratic values, to the conviction that democracy is merely a vehicle that the FIS will cynically use to come to power and then eliminate: "one man, one vote...one time." Anecdotes abound. FIS slogans reportedly include such statements as "A vote against FIS is a vote against God"; "God and the Prophet have said No to any national Charter and to a Constitution" *(La Mithaq wa la Dastur, qall Allah wa'l-Rasul)*. A young leader of the FIS, Shaykh Jaballah, has rejected new constitutional provisions on plurality and democracy as alien to the "Islamicness" of the Algerian people, and an "intrusion in the disguise of secularism."[3] On the other hand, although the party was clearly divided over the wisdom of participating in elections in 1991, for example—given the state's arrest of the FIS top leadership—the leadership nonetheless did opt for electoral participation, and proceeded to organize and campaign hard and successfully. In

---

[3]See Boutheina Cheriet, "Islamism and Feminism," in John C. Entelis and Phillip C. Naylor (eds.), *State and Society in Algeria*, Boulder, CO: Westview, 1992, p. 202.

short, quotations abound for all those who justify either an acceptance or a rejection of the FIS agenda.

Most observers draw some distinction between the top leader of the FIS, 'Abbasi Madani, and his deputy 'Ali Belhaj. Madani is in his early sixties, is a professor of comparative education at the University of Algiers, and is known for his superb command of classical Arabic and his oratorical ability; he obtained his Ph.D. at London University's Institute of Education. He has "breathed new life into the classic Islamic critique of Western political thought."[4]   He is viewed as a moderate within FIS circles, one who confirms the need for democracy for Algeria and other Western political values "as long as they are not inconsistent with the Shari'a."[5] Yet this last condition set by Madani, typical of many Islamists, leaves the statement open to the widest interpretation; after all, the Qur'an and the Shari'a are widely debated within the Islamic world as to whether they provide an intellectual foundation for democracy or against it. Madani's deputy, 'Ali Belhaj, is in his late thirties, is a schoolteacher and an imam, and is widely known as a radical, fiery orator. He and Madani have coexisted and worked together in the FIS for several years, despite ideological differences. The statement is widely attributed to Belhaj that "there is no democracy in Islam." In the end, one might as well speculate about whether Christian or Judaic texts "reveal a democratic spirit" or not; the question is simply not answerable in the abstract. FIS policies will ultimately be revealed by their actions, under circumstances not now foreseeable; this is not a reassuring statement, but not much more can be said of most other untested political parties in Algeria either.

In my view, then, the question of FIS commitment to democracy remains an open one; it is not a foregone conclusion that the FIS will eliminate Algerian democracy—something that has barely ever existed and does not now exist under the junta. Moderate Islamists see

---

[4]Cheriet, p. 178.

[5]This proviso is typical of most Islamists, and indeed represents the nub of the argument as to how much the Shari'a might "override" other democratic principles; Islamists in the Muslim world differ profoundly along a broad spectrum as to what this means. Many Islamists say that they accept the fact that the people can vote Islamists out of power, because such an act would mean that the Islamists had failed in their task, i.e., Islam cannot fail, but Islamists and their policies can fail.

some benefits and values in aspects of democratic practice—at least in principle; whether they or any other Algerian group will continue to see advantages in democracy under the pressures of power is quite open to question.

Nonetheless, whatever one may say theoretically about the FIS's approach to democratic practice, there is no doubt that it has been willing to participate in numerous elections, both at the municipal and national level. The showing was impressive as the FIS won many municipalities in the 1990 elections—Algeria's first ever—and in which virtually no violence took place and few charges of vote rigging were reported. The FIS won 55 percent of the 1,541 communal assemblies and 32 of the 48 *wilayat*, or provinces, capturing 54 percent of the popular vote in the process.[6]

A further revealing test of Islamist parties is their functioning in municipal governments. The significance of the experience is much debated.[7] Many believe it showed dangerous features, citing instances of use of local power to strengthen their own followings—yet this is characteristic of most political parties anywhere. The FIS did make tentative efforts to implement the Shari'a in various places at different times. For example:

> FIS-controlled communes passed measures to ban the wearing of shorts in Tipasa, end the mixing of girls and boys in schools in Constantine, cancel a popular *rai* [Arab rock] festival in Oran, and reject any correspondence to the local administration in Jijel not ﹐written in Arabic.[8]

Incidents of the hassling of unveiled women are mentioned—it is unclear whether these were authorized or spontaneous and independent acts. Other accounts state that the municipal government

---

[6]Bradford Dillman, "Transition to Democracy in Algeria," in John C. Entelis and Phillip C. Naylor (eds.), *State and Society in Algeria*, Boulder, CO: Westview, 1992, p. 35.

[7]It can be argued that municipal governance, or provincial (regional) governance, provides a good venue for observing the reality of the ruling style of radical parties. But the local experience is not totally determinative; for example, communists have ruled cities and regions in both Italy and India for years, coming in and out of power legally. Yet there would not have been great confidence about the communist party's intentions in either place if it had come to national power.

[8]Dillman, p. 39.

budgets under the FIS were starved by the FLN-controlled central government in order to render them ineffective. Elsewhere in the resort town of Tipasa, the FIS reportedly actually did nothing to prevent mixed bathing at beaches that are popular local attractions. In the end, the experience of FIS management of municipal governments seemed not to support dire predictions about draconian social approaches. The FIS may be politically unsophisticated in terms of national policies, but like Islamists elsewhere in the Muslim world, they have their thumb on the pulse of real life in the neighborhoods—the wants, needs, and problems, and they try to support real-world social programs to alleviate the worst of the problems. They are thus not without experience in budgets, administration of programs, grass-roots organization, etc.

One mistake in analyzing Islamist movements is to assume that they are static in outlook and behavior. In fact, Islamists in the Muslim world as a whole are undergoing a gradual process of evolution and even major political education. As one observer remarked to me in Morocco, the demand of a local Islamist movement for application of the Qur'an as a means of bringing about social justice must be understood in context: most of these young Islamists have no model from which to draw concepts of social justice other than the Islamic tradition. It is not surprising, then, that this should be the first recourse for Islamists concerned about social realities and seeking answers. Other Islamists[9] have come to recognize that certain Western political values such as human rights and limitation of the power of the central government are values that in fact can directly apply to the position of Islamists today; they are the ones, after all, who are repressed, tortured, and killed without due process. Many of them are coming to the realization that while democracy can never guarantee that the Islamists will come to power, it can guarantee that they will stay alive and able to propagate their message into the future.

In the final analysis, two factors are likely to determine the FIS approach to democratic governance: the circumstances under which it comes to power, and the developing political culture of the state. The odds, based on regional experience and Algerian political culture

---

[9]In various interviews I have conducted over the past few years with Islamists.

to date, do not strongly favor democratic governance. Algeria is not unique in this. But it must begin the process. Only through exposure to the realities of running a state will the more moderate Islamists gain greater wisdom and experience. Radical elements may never be convinced, and may present a problem to the state until they are marginalized. And only the public's exposure to the strengths and weaknesses of Islamist rule will break its often blind faith that somehow the Islamists have all the answers. FIS support had reportedly dropped in the interim between the 1990 municipal elections and the 1991 national elections, based in part on some public recognition that they indeed did not have all the answers, and had implemented some bad ones as well as some good ones.

The Islamists may not be the ideal next regime for Algeria, but there is no getting around their formidable presence and role in society. The failure of past regimes, a one-time plurality of public support for the FIS in 1991, and a hideous civil conflict stemming from the refusal to honor the results of that FIS plurality in the national elections have all left Algeria with very little else than to deal with this reality.

CULTURAL ISSUES

Islamist movements are deeply concerned about culture—the next most important thing after power. For it is Islamic culture that helps define what Islamists want. Islamists therefore talk about three stages of independence. The first stage was political independence, achieved when the foreign colonialists and imperialists were driven from the country. The second stage is liberation of the country's economic resources from foreign control, typified by the nationalization of gas and oil companies and other natural resources; this too has been a reality for some time. The third stage is the recapturing of the country's own authentic culture from the "cultural control" of former colonial masters or of the West in general.[10] This task entails the removal of regimes that came to power at the time of formal independence that were typified by native leaders who, while liberators, were also profoundly stamped by the colonial mold of Western education, secularism, and lack of regard for traditional values, in-

---

[10]Burgat, p. 4.

cluding Islam. The FLN has been perceived as precisely such a party—thoroughly spiritually bankrupt in its drift away from Algerian culture—a shortcoming perhaps only recently being amended in the party's new face.[11]

As noted in Chapter One, Islamists have often been critical of Arab nationalism because it enshrined a secular trend in Arab politics. Indeed, the very idea of nationalism is Western in origin and linked with the concept of the nation-state; that idea is arbitrarily, and hence only weakly, developed in the Arab world, where all are "Arabs." But in more recent years there has been some rapprochement, with the Islamists recognizing the value of Arab nationalism to the overall project of recapturing cultural authenticity—as long as the secularists abandon their insistence on the secular expression of nationalism. This fusion of nationalism and Islam will very likely play a greater role in the future.[12] Indeed, in its foreign policy outlook, Arab nationalism and Islamism bear a close resemblance.

We can, therefore, posit that the FIS will embrace the full range of Algerian nationalism in its policies, even while sympathetic to the broader project of Islamization throughout the Muslim world. Indeed, the FIS is likely to be ultranationalist—at least toward the West—since it perceives a key cultural divide between the powerful West and the weaker Muslim world. This gulf is not Islam versus Christianity, but Islam versus colonial power, military power, Western "arrogance" and domination, as well as opposition to what they perceive not as a Christian but an amoral Western value system.

LANGUAGE

The language issue is a critical feature of the cultural struggle. The Islamists strongly stress the resuscitation of classical or formal Arabic in the education system, over the use of the local Algerian Arabic dialect. Interestingly, they also strongly favor the adoption of English over French as the country's second official language, since English is regarded as culturally "neutral" compared to French, laden as it is

---

[11]Other leaders seen by the Islamists in this same light are Nasser in Egypt, Bourguiba in Tunisia, the Shah in Iran, and Zulfikar Ali Bhutto in Pakistan, among others.

[12]Burgat, pp. 29–30.

with the triple baggage of its colonial past, its pervasive presence among the secularized elite today, and its close associations with France. English bears none of this historical burden—at least in Algeria—and would also open up Algeria more truly to international and technical circles that are increasingly English-oriented. Here the Islamists exhibit the interest typical of most Islamist movements in technological advancement—yet somehow without accepting all the social and philosophical implications of modern technological society, including the questioning of all authority and a thoroughgoing secularism.

For obvious reasons, this issue has direct implications for the large French-speaking elite that sees its political, social, and economic situation directly threatened by the Arabizing outlook—this includes the military, which sees itself as second to none in the defense of nationalism but a large part of which is francophone.

The FIS in power will therefore continue to emphasize the teaching of Arabic, not only as the national language but as the vehicle of Islam. More positions will undoubtedly be allocated to Arabic speakers within the bureaucracy in place of those dominated today by French speakers. As we noted earlier, this is in part a continuation of a decades-old FLN campaign, in which the use of French in public signs—even street signs—was eliminated in favor of Arabic. Those educated in French may find the language to be of diminishing advantage in the face of likely affirmative action for Arabic-educated students.

MORALITY

FIS rule will almost certainly witness the application of stricter rules of public decorum regarding clothing for men and women, especially women. While radical Islamists, such as Belhaj, have advocated the return of women to the home, it is unlikely that the FIS will implement such a measure. First, the economy cannot afford to have Algerian women leave the workplace, where they are already importantly engaged. Second, families cannot afford the loss of income through loss of widespread employment by wives. Third, most Islamists in general have not banned women from working, nor is it in their philosophy to do so; the important thing is maintenance of decorum and respect for women, often in separated institutions or offices.[13] In Iran and Sudan today, women play a significant role in the economy. There, women's dress codes do require wearing of the full head-scarf; women also work separately from men where practical.

The Shari'a will very likely be imposed to some extent under the FIS in Algeria, particularly in areas of family law, which most women see as discriminatory and unequal in treatment. This feature is not new, in that the Algerian parliament—under not FIS but FLN dominance—passed a Family Law in 1984 that was based considerably upon the Shari'a—particularly in areas relating to inheritance and ease of male-initiated divorce. Women have sought to undo this legislation—as they have fought it in many other Muslim countries. (In Saudi Arabia it is nearly fully applied.) It is a virtual certitude that the FIS in power will perpetuate this law, and perhaps extend it. On the other hand, it is worth noting that in the Islamic Republic of Iran there has been consistent reform of divorce laws away from the Shari'a in ways that greatly strengthen women's position in divorce and other legal procedures. In fact there is a contradiction between *traditionalists* in Islam who are more literalist than the Islamists in interpreting the Qur'an and the Shari'a. The FIS may well find itself striking certain kinds of compromises on these issues over time, especially since there is a trend within Islamist thought that sees full application of the Shari'a not as an imperative, but as a long-range project, consistent with conditions.[14]

The FIS will undoubtedly seek to bring penal law as well into closer concordance with the Shari'a, but it is uncertain whether it will be applied literally and fully, i.e., stoning of adulterers, amputation of hands for thieves, etc. Even in Saudi Arabia these punishments are not applied indiscriminately, and even less so in Iran. Again, some trends in Islamic thought regard these Shari'a penalties *(hudud)* as really applicable only in the ideal Muslim state where the population has already attained a high material and moral level and is no longer

---

[13]It is interesting to note that in Mexico City, metro cars are set aside exclusively for women during the rush hour to protect them from being hassled by men in crowded cars. The Catholic moralist realism thus coincides with the Islamist.

[14]See Roy, p. 38.

confronted with grinding social problems that fray the moral fabric and push people toward violations of the law.

The sale of alcohol will almost surely be banned in public places. Whether the regime will single-mindedly root alcohol out everywhere is doubtful—based on the precedent of private (underground) use in Saudi Arabia, Pakistan, Iran, and Sudan. Films and television will undoubtedly be subject to censorship, as they are in many other non-Islamist Muslim states.

While Westerners (and many Algerians) may not find congenial the kinds of moral codes that the FIS might apply, austerity is usually the hallmark of most revolutionary regimes following a drastic change. These codes are furthermore not atypical of the conservative codes of several Gulf states, Pakistan and elsewhere. The pattern would suggest that many regimes are moving toward more conservative norms in order to seek to gain Islamic legitimacy, but that over time the demands of both efficacy and need for public acceptance of these norms will force more pragmatic and even more liberalized practice. The process may take many decades to work through—or more, depending on the societies and social processes in question. These issues really represent the internal problems of the states in question—unless, of course, they should fall into the category of consistent gross violations of basic human rights. But if it is primarily a question of *austere* law, equitably and juridically applied, it becomes a more difficult target for international human rights activists when compared to arbitrary and illegal regime actions that exist around the globe.

THE BERBERS, THE FIS, AND POTENTIAL SEPARATISM

Berber aspirations and concerns will make up an important issue in the future development of Algerian politics, especially if the FIS should come to power. A high proportion of the Berbers have been outspoken against the FIS because they fear that it will intensify Islamization policies that many see as synonymous with Arabization.[15]

---

[15]Hardly all Berbers are anti-FIS: the FIS received the second-highest vote in Kabylia (the Berber region) after the FFS, the so-called Berber party; a number of leading Islamist figures within the FIS are from the Kabylia, according to FIS spokesman

As we noted in Chapter One, the Berbers, through their Berber Cultural Movement, have sought a constitutional amendment to make their language, Tamazight, the second official language of the country after Arabic. Because of significant Berber opposition to the FIS, the Berbers have been singled out for special support by anti-FIS elements within the regime. In September 1995 the junta actually declared Berber to be an obligatory course for *all* students in 17 provinces, even where Berbers are not always a majority and where Arabs might object. This tactic presents its own problems, since it involves the strengthening of a separate cultural identity—the promotion of divisiveness—among Berbers, which potentially could present the future Algerian state with a growing ethnic problem if mishandled.

The two leading Berber parties, The Socialist Forces Front (FFS) and the Rally for Culture and Democracy (RCD), take radically different positions on the FIS issue, however, since the FFS—while opposing the FIS—believes that only through integration of the Islamists into the political system can civil war and strife be avoided.[16] The RCD, much the weaker of the two parties among the Berbers—and some would say a creature of the regime—remains militantly anti-FIS and opposed to its participation in government in any way.

Despite significant Berber opposition to the FIS, it should not be assumed that the Berbers are anti-Islamic; on the contrary, their Islamic identity remains very strong. To Berbers, the Islamic identity in fact supersedes the Arab one, which is why they strongly oppose linkage of Islamization with Arabization—utterly distinct categories in their view. Islamic practice thus remains strong among Berbers. Ironically, such Islamist support as exists in the Berber stronghold of Kabylia is represented by the radical militant Armed Islamic Group (GIA), which is outside of the FIS entirely and opposes any compromise with the regime short of total victory. The Kabylia region is a

---

Anwar Haddam—including 'Abbasi Madani, Shaykh Muhammad Sa'id, and the earlier Islamist activist Shaykh Bin Badis (never actually in the FIS itself).

[16]Based on interviews with the FFS in Algiers in 1993. In fact, in my view, the FFS has the most intelligent, realistic, and farsighted view of the dilemma of Algerian politics today of any party in the country.

particularly sensitive one in Algerian history as a source of resistance and intellectual leadership.[17]

The Berber issue has taken on a regional dimension with the public support of King Hassan of Morocco for Berber linguistic rights in Algeria, in keeping with his own successful cultural policies toward Berber rights in Morocco.[18] Given general tensions between Morocco and Algeria, the king's pronouncements are resented by the Algerian regime—as were his remarks in 1991 disapproving the annulment of the FIS victory and his comments that it would have been instructive to see just how the FIS would actually have conducted itself in power.[19]

The FIS itself seems not to have taken a fully clear position on the Berber issue. The FIS strongly supports Arabization, that is, propagation of Arabic over French, as a return to the authentic cultural roots of Algeria. But it is not at all clear that this general policy explicitly supports imposition of Arabic on the Berbers. FIS spokesman Anwar Haddam states that FIS supports the right of Berbers to education in their own language. Thus, FIS policies might not explicitly threaten the status of Tamazight, but do threaten the position of Francophones within Algerian society, among whom the Berbers rank very high.

The issue is of immense importance to the FIS, since it relates to broader policies of Islamist movements toward ethnic minorities in general. In principle, Islamist ideology has no inclination toward ethnic chauvinism *among Muslims.* On the contrary, Islamists strongly oppose ethnic differences that divide Muslims; they always press in the direction of a higher order of unity among all Muslims, even leading some of the most radical Islamists to a virtual rejection of Arab nationalist ideology as competitive with Islamism. Algerian Islamists thus have no belief in principle in the superiority of Arabs

---

[17]See "Algeria: Is the Berber Backlash Beginning?" *Mideast Mirror*, September 26, 1994, pp. 16–19.

[18]Ibid., p. 18.

[19]Liberal Algerians somewhat bitterly respond to outsiders who speak of how "interesting" it might have been to see just what the FIS would actually do in power, "Thank you, but we don't want to be your social laboratory."

over Berbers. But Arabization as an *anti-French* policy has direct, if unintended, impact on Berbers, creating Berber opposition to it.[20]

Future policies of the FIS toward the Berbers will be very important for the future stability of Algeria. The chances are that the FIS will be tolerant toward the Tamazight language, even while strengthening Arabic at the expense of French. The issue of the French language, as we have noted, is not just a linguistic but a cultural and even class issue that has proved highly divisive in Algeria's modern history; no other regional state has the same problem with French to the same divisive degree—despite slight overtones of cultural superiority among French speakers in Tunisia, Morocco, and Lebanon as well. Anti-French-language policies obviously also affect Algerian relations with Paris, both psychologically and in practice, partially explaining French hostility to the FIS. This would not, of course, be the first time Algeria has engaged in a campaign against French.

Given the considerable degree of French and secular education among the Berbers, they will basically be uncomfortable with FIS rule and a probable source of opposition through their existing political parties. The FIS may therefore treat Kabylia as a center of anti-FIS sentiment. It is also a region that France could be tempted to manipulate against FIS rule in Algeria in the event of a serious break-

---

[20]The Islamist record on ethnic issues is mixed in other states. In Sudan a harsh Arabization campaign has been under way in the south, but the Sudanese south is also non-Muslim and mostly animist in faith, a religious form theologically unacceptable in Islam (unlike Islam's view of Christianity as sharing common roots with Islam). Thus ethnic policies in Sudan are readily entwined with religious ones—as well as with state fears for the division of the country. Discrimination in the south predates Islamist policies, but has been intensified by them. In Iran, the clerical regime has been barely tolerant of non-Persian languages—even among fellow Shi'ite Azerbaijanis—mainly out of fear of potential separatist trends that can emerge from active linguistic autonomy; but the Shah had no tolerance for minority culture. Iranian Islamists have also acted harshly against the religiously heterodox Baha'i community, however, and troubles have even cropped up with the Sunni minority in Iran. In Pakistan, there has been broad tolerance among Islamists for languages spoken by Muslim ethnic groups (Pashtuns, Sindhis, Baluch) other than the dominant Punjabi, but total intolerance toward the Ahmadi sect—an utterly unorthodox Islamic offshoot that Muslims view as heretical. In Turkey, Islamists have claimed that Turkey in fact should be united on the basis of Islam rather than on the Turkish ethnicity that excludes the large Kurdish minority. In the Arab world, the issue seems to be complicated by the fact that Arabic is the actual language of the Qur'an and of mainstream Islamic religious discourse since the beginning, thus linking the religious factor to ethnic and linguistic factors perhaps more than is intended.

down of relations between the two states. Berber loyalty to a FIS regime could become quite questionable, depending on FIS policies, a fact that makes Kabylia and the Berber region a highly sensitive one. The manipulation of the Berbers already by anti-FIS elements within the regime suggests that they would be hard put to stay out of a future struggle against the FIS unless the FIS itself develops highly enlightened policies toward the Berbers. If internal movements should undertake armed opposition to a FIS regime, Kabylia might be a natural gravitation point for them. While an actual Berber bid for separation would seem quite unlikely now, extreme exacerbation of the Berber issue, coupled with potential external manipulation (France, Morocco, Tunisia, Libya, or even Egypt), disastrous policies by the FIS, and ongoing civil war could all combine to eventually push the Berbers toward an independence movement. The Berber question thus remains a critical one for the FIS and Algeria's future and is likely to take on greater salience rather than less in the years ahead.

THE PRESENCE OF FOREIGNERS IN ALGERIA

The violent Islamist Bouyali group in the mid-1980s called for the withdrawal of all French peace corps and technical assistance workers, and even more interestingly, the return of all emigrants back to Algeria from France.[21,22] The GIA, under conditions of virtual civil war today, has threatened the lives of all foreigners assisting the Algerian state and has killed over forty of them—often slitting their throats. The French have made up 30 percent of those foreigners killed,[23] but many other nationalities have been targeted as well, including Italians, Russians, British and Yugoslavs—but surprisingly, so far no Americans. A high proportion of these operations were carried out by the non-FIS GIA.

---

[21]See Burgat, p. 267. This is an excellent source book on the topic, with valuable interviews and long quotes from Islamist leaders, giving some sense of their thinking. The translation by William McDowell is unfortunately quite bad—literal, muddy, and confusing.

[22]It is interesting that the FIS also talks about the possibility of attracting large numbers of Algerians back from France by encouraging economic growth in Algeria.

[23]*Mideast Mirror*, October 10, 1994, p. 12.

The FIS, even in times of severe violence in Algeria, has refrained from an explicit policy of attacking foreigners and has sought to avoid alienating external powers who potentially can be of assistance to them, now or in the future. Foreigners in any case would mostly comprise specialists, technicians, and businessmen. FIS rhetoric would seem to have a different agenda than declaration of war against the external world—although the multiplicity of groups within the FIS makes it difficult to generalize too broadly. FIS rhetoric does not talk today about the need to eliminate foreign expertise and business ties. Mainstream FIS ideology carries little overtones of cultural xenophobia, or "war against the world." It is therefore unlikely that the FIS will *deliberately* adopt any policy that seeks to remove foreigners from the country—at what will almost certainly be considerable economic and technical cost.

This does not mean that the FIS might not adopt policies that will have the inadvertent effect of encouraging most foreigners to leave. Like Saudi Arabia, Algeria has never encouraged tourism, and under a FIS regime, foreigners without a pressing reason to visit may shun it entirely. Algeria's beaches may languish under new moral codes, and night life will be nonexistent. But the FIS will not wish to alienate necessary foreign expertise and presence, and those needed foreigners are unlikely to leave simply because of Islamist austerity. After all, tens of thousands of foreigners live under austere conditions in Saudi Arabia quite willingly when it is important to their jobs or businesses. It is an environment of violence and insecurity that will most likely bring about a foreign exodus. If power-sharing arrangements between the FIS and other groups are unstable, and merely represent a formal truce while a violent struggle for power goes on in the background—akin to the conditions today—few foreigners are likely to risk the situation. Or if the FIS in power cannot establish security, either because of the activities of its enemies or because of internal factional struggle, such chaos will be extremely deleterious to a continued presence of foreign expertise and commercial ties. The FIS will desperately require technological, financial, and commercial ties with the West if only to implement its own social programs; there are few grounds therefore for anticipating a deliberate xenophobic campaign unless the West should adopt an entirely hostile attitude toward the FIS in its struggle with the current junta regime.

ECONOMIC POLICIES

More basic questions remain about future FIS policies toward economic questions affecting both the domestic and the international economy. The first is the economic philosophy of the FIS: is it liberal-free market, or centralized-statist? Is it radical or revisionist in terms of the international order? It is important to look at the (limited) FIS statements on this issue, look at precedents set by other Islamist parties in power, and to analyze the economic pressures a new FIS regime would face in power.

One interesting indicator is FIS support in the preelection for President Chadli's FLN reformist policies that focused on liberalization of the economy and a lessening role for the state in the economic sector. Of course, the imperatives of raw tactical politics should not be ignored here: the FIS naturally focused on the FLN's past economic failures to meet people's needs—especially in view of the state's huge income from control of massive gas reserves. The FIS also had tactical reasons to applaud policies that helped wrench the FLN hand away from the levers of economic power—as a way of weakening the FLN in general. Indeed, one characteristic has dominated FIS policymaking all along: a pragmatic approach to many issues with a fine eye to electoral pressures. One term for this is "opportunism"; another is "pragmatism" or responsiveness to reality—as politicians are supposed to do.

Most Islamist parties in the Middle East in fact generally oppose strong statist economic policies,[24] reflecting an Islamic tradition supportive of private property, the market, and commerce as an honorable pursuit.[25] The current social origin of these movements' supporters—commercial, petty bourgeois or lower-middle-class groups, traditional businessmen—would also encourage the economic conservatism of Islamist ideology per se. These conservative instincts represent a broad and fundamental reality within political

---

[24]Among Algeria's Islamist parties and groups, only the Nahda Party has actually advocated policies supportive of the state sector in opposition to broad privatization—unusual for an Islamist party.

[25]By contrast, Christianity, for the better part of its history, and Confucianism have had little regard for the mercantile tradition.

Islam.[26]   Yet, the general programs and statements of the FIS notwithstanding, this study contends that the party is likely to be rather statist in its policies upon taking power—even if not to the extreme degree of former FLN rule. The reasons are many.

First, the political culture of Muslim states has a powerful impact on the conduct and policies of all parties within the country; it would be surprising if it were otherwise. Algerian political culture, as noted earlier, has nurtured perhaps the most powerful statist tradition in the Arab world. That experience has already shaped the perceptions, experience, and perhaps even the expectations of the bulk of the population. True, many Algerian political parties, including the Islamists, have criticized FLN statist policies, but they will be hard put to bring about a radical transformation of economic philosophy overnight, even if the will exists.

Second, the massive gas and oil sector of the country creates the most fundamental political-economic reality for any Algerian government. Energy resources over most of the world almost by definition belong to the state sector and are extremely unlikely to be privatized. One key reason is that control of the oil and gas sector is the mainstay of state power, creating a powerful predisposition for any regime not to weaken any state control over such a key sector of the economy. A new FIS regime would therefore be extremely unlikely to dispossess itself of economic instruments of state power. Since gas constitutes the vast bulk of state revenue, the very existence of a massive energy-based economy overshadows any other potentially productive sector of the economy.

Third, the FIS will almost surely encourage private enterprise in the service and small manufacturing sector, but it is unlikely to engage in major privatization at a time when its assertion of control over state and society in general is politically urgent. One cannot envision a period of "one hundred days" in which the FIS would seek to turn around the very foundations of the economic system. If it ever does

---

[26] It is notable, for example, that the Islamic Republic of Iran has found a consistently key base of support among the bazaari class of lower-middle-class merchants; the same goes for Sudan. Iran nonetheless also has a bloated state sector that has become the special preserve of hard-line clergy—not on an ideological basis, but as a source of income for their line of political activities.

so, it will do so reluctantly and under external pressure, just like virtually every single other state in the Middle East, of any political stripe. Despite its philosophical awareness that the FLN's statist policies were a failure, the FIS will be politically unwilling to cede economic power to other elements in the society who could use that power to mount a political threat. It will at the same time—very much as in Iran and Sudan—be likely to funnel state business, purchasing requirements, etc., to elements of the Islamist bourgeoisie in order to retain their support. This sort of bourgeoisie thus often become compromised—as in Turkey, Iran, Egypt, and elsewhere—by dependency on deals they receive via political ties to the state rather than through free competition in the market place.

A fourth reality will be the need to meet urgent economic and social needs among the population. Expectations from the population for major change under FIS rule will be high: demands for food, housing, and jobs is extraordinary in a country with over 30 percent unemployment already. A FIS regime will be under great pressure to quickly adopt populist economic policies and make a dramatic break with past failures by the FLN to meet the needs of the masses. The FIS will need to ensure the continuing support of the population and to implement the FIS vision of social justice. These needs, too, suggest a requirement for maximum FIS control over the economic levers of the state in order to implement the urgent social agenda they espouse and have long reflected in their social work in the poorer quarters of Algerian cities.

Thus, this study argues that the FIS will be compelled by tradition, events, and political dynamics to move in a statist direction, even if it has no particular philosophical brief for such policies per se. A number of FIS statements additionally suggest a certain ambivalence about the state's role in the economy. FIS spokesman Anwar Haddam laudably speaks of the need for the state to diversify the economy away from exclusive dependence on gas and oil, particularly by emphasizing the agricultural sector. Stimulation of the agricultural sector will be an important step toward the FIS goal of agricultural self-sufficiency—a critical goal, considering that 80 percent of government-subsidized agricultural items are imported. But the FIS also seeks to build a healthier domestic economy less dependent upon the external world, especially the West. The FIS seeks to diversify the economy by strengthening economic ties with the Maghreb regime for a start, in order to bargain with the West from a stronger position of a more regionally integrated economy. Haddam admits that such a policy will require some degree of governmental interference in the economy in the initial stages of reorientation. These goals, too, then suggest that the role of the state in the economy is likely to be very strong, even though the FIS explicitly eschews a state-controlled economy in principle.

The FIS interest in seeking a more integrated regional, i.e., Maghrebi economy may make greater political than economic sense as well. The states of the Maghreb are not highly complementary in the structure of their economies and are highly competitive in the economic sector. A political will can perhaps improve the development of a regional economy, but states like Morocco and Tunisia are likely to be much more intent on building bilateral economic relations with the European Union than with Algeria on a political basis.

The FIS likewise looks for investment from the West, and seeks greater industrialization. But it is also naturally concerned about what free-market relations with the European Union might do. If the industrial sector of the Maghreb is integrated into Europe, Maghrebi industry is likely to be devastated by European competition. At the same time, the FIS is naturally unwilling to allow itself to simply become the site for "polluting industries" that are no longer welcome in Europe and best exported to the Maghreb. Contradictions exist here too, then, in FIS economic policy.

Finally we have the question of FIS dealings with international institutions like the IMF. Haddam comments that the IMF is basically an institution that has no genuine interest in the development of Third World economies, but is primarily an instrument to ensure the payment of debt back to the industrialized lenders. He questions the soundness of IMF policies even as development policies. The FIS may therefore be reluctant to embrace IMF formulas for debt payment and economic restructuring. Such views spring not from any particular Islamist outlook, but are typical of the views of many Third World states that harbor suspicions about the international economic order. The FIS will reportedly meet its international economic obligations, although at this time it suggests that the economic commitments of the junta since 1992 are illegal. One suspects that this issue might be negotiable down the road.[27]

The FIS in power is also likely to draw on the network of international Islamist banking based in Saudi Arabia and the Gulf. The Saudi al-Baraka bank long assisted the National Islamic Front in Sudan and would clearly do so in Algeria unless it adopted egregiously anti-Saudi policies—which is unlikely. The FIS has maintained fairly good ties with Saudi Arabia, despite FIS support for Saddam Hussein in the Gulf War over Kuwait. Saudi Arabia will seek to bring an Islamist Algeria into its own circle rather than let it drift toward common cause with Iran; financial ties are a key Saudi instrument in this regard.

GAS AND OIL

There should be little doubt that any Algerian regime will continue to sell its gas to all customers: there has been no hint of anything to the contrary in any of its pronouncements. It will have deep economic needs that only the sale of energy can meet. Indeed, there has been no case among any of the most radical Middle Eastern regimes of politicizing oil sales policy—not in Libya, Iran, or Iraq—and all have worked extremely well with foreign oil companies, including American ones, even during the height of state-to-state political crises. Interdependency is simply too high. Nonetheless, FIS spokesmen have spoken of the need for "fair prices" on energy, suggesting that Algeria would join the ranks of energy producers who seek higher prices—in opposition to the longer-range Saudi tactic of modest

---

[27]Yet even here, the policies of the Sudanese National Islamic Front in power are instructive. The government, under heavy pressure from the IMF on debts (from past regimes), actually went to great lengths to implement IMF recommendations on austerity in many areas. Rather than succumbing at the time to a generalized denunciation of the "Western-dominated international financial order" or "imperialist-controlled policies of the IMF," the Sudanese regime introduced much privatization, cut many subsidies on consumer goods, reduced the bureaucracy, and implemented other recommended IMF policies through a highly businesslike Minister of Finance. It was only later on, when other aspects of Sudan's domestic and international policies began to displease Western and many Middle Eastern states, that the IMF politically begin to harden its line toward Khartoum, leading to ill will and a political rupture between the two.

prices. Pressures for higher gas and oil prices are likely to emerge from most producer nations in the years ahead, given their increasing financial needs, but of course the market cannot be that simply manipulated. But Algeria under the FIS will be at least as nationalistic as it was under the FLN—and maybe more so—in its determination to gain "fair prices." A cutoff of gas to its European customers is conceivable only under circumstances of extreme confrontation between the two sides—which is unlikely.

At the same time, the present regime has been pursuing foreign investment, particularly in the energy sector—including a $1 billion participation agreement with ARCO, suggesting a desire to move ahead in privatization in certain areas. While the energy sector is probably a highly attractive field of investment for foreign capital, only a clear sign of Algerian political and social stability will be likely to attract capital in other areas. That is not a predictable condition for Algeria for the foreseeable future.

In the end, then, FIS economic policies are not likely to be ideologically driven, but there are many good reasons to assume that it will be more statist than it presently claims—or even intends—and will be prickly on issues of IMF debt schedules and other arrangements with European financial institutions.

DIFFERENCES AMONG ISLAMIST GROUPS

The FIS, despite its position as the central political grouping for most Algerian Islamist movements, does not have a monopoly on Islamist politics in the country; two other Islamist parties are also active on the scene and differ in their political goals and tactical means. While none of these parties can begin to approach the political clout of the FIS, their views are important. First, they broaden the spectrum of Islamist thinking—a particularly critical factor when radical Islamist groups tend to seek an ideological monopoly over defining "what is Islam." Second, their views could come to have weight in the future, especially where they are more liberal or realistic—useful to a secular regime seeking some Islamist representation without including the FIS.

Hamas

Hamas as a political party was founded in 1990 by Shaykh Mahfoudh Nahnah, growing out of his earlier nonpolitical movement Al-Irshad wa'l-Islah (Guidance and Reform). Its name was directly inspired by the Palestinian radical Islamist group of the same name, although the Algerian version is not radical. Its strongest ideological affiliation is with the Muslim Brotherhood movement, and specifically its left wing. Hamas in its origins is part of a broader wing of Islamist thinking often referred to as *tabligh,* or propagation of the faith. It emphasizes the need for society to undergo considerable moral education and moral advancement before it becomes practical to think of introducing Islam as a *political* force, much less taking political power. In other words, it stresses an evolutionary approach to moral change, rather than a revolutionary one that would utilize state power to impose Islamic beliefs.

While the Hamas movement has now indeed become a political party seeking power, its outlook is conditioned by its emergence from the *tabligh* tradition. It is more "principled" than the FIS, that is, specific principles, more than tactical considerations, guide its activities. It accepts democratic principles as an essential element of the Algerian system and eschews violence. More than any other Islamist group, it has been willing to consider cooperation with the ruling Algerian junta in the interests of reaching a settlement. Its leader, Mahfoudh Nahnah, ran as one of three opposition candidates for the presidency in the November 1995 elections, otherwise boycotted by all the other leading parties. Nahnah won 25 percent of the vote, and could be included—even named prime minister—in a new government as a result of his willingness to work with the regime.[28] Like all Islamist groups, however, Hamas knows it cannot afford to reach accommodation with a regime intent on the broader destruction of the FIS—despite the deep rivalry between the two parties.[29] Hamas, as a moderate Islamist organization, plays one of the most important Islamist political roles in Algeria after the FIS. It is a mod-

---

[28]*Mideast Mirror,* November 22, 1995, p. 16.

[29]Hugh Roberts, "A Trial of Strength: Algerian Islamism," in James Piscatori (ed.), *Islamic Fundamentalism and the Gulf Crisis,* Chicago: American Academy of Arts and Sciences, 1991, pp. 136–137.

erating factor, a bridge between the junta and the FIS; the respect that Shaykh Nahnah enjoys is important to the party's position, but the party seeks to transcend mere personality.

Al-Nahda (Renaissance)

Originally a clandestine movement founded in 1974 by Shaykh 'Abdallah Jaballah, al-Nahda became a legal political party in 1990. Like Hamas, it springs from the Muslim Brotherhood tradition, although not directly linked to it. It is on the left wing of the Islamic spectrum in its opposition to economic reform via liberalization of the economy and its support for the state sector. This position on the left of the FIS enables it to ideologically challenge the more centrist FIS views on economic issues. Its views are more intellectually coherent—and hence less tactical in nature. Its following is, however, quite modest, and somewhat regionally based.[30]

Al-Nahda's positions further demonstrate the existence of an Islamist spectrum on various issues, including the left. Contrary to Western popular beliefs in the rigidity of Islamist thinking, there is no reason why political Islam itself should not have an ideological spectrum. Iranian movements in political Islam (albeit Shi'ite) in the late 1970s also demonstrated left-wing movements, especially the Mojahedin-e-Khalq that was strongly influenced by a quasi-Marxist vision of history; the Mojahedin spoke of a struggle of the oppressed against unjust and ungodly power, in which Islam would represent a revolutionary force designed to bring revolution and millenarian social and economic change on a new religious basis of justice. Violence and force were perceived as necessary instruments of that struggle. Other Iranian Islamist movements also had powerful reformist visions involving the use of state power to bring about social justice.

These movements, however, are less common within Sunni political Islam, where more traditional views of civil society and the role of traditional commercial classes dominate. Iran today is torn uncomfortably between more populist, statist structures on the one hand, and reliance upon traditional bazaari classes with traditional views of a limited state role in the ownership of the means of production on

---

[30]Roberts (1991), pp. 137–138.

the other. These themes bear watching in Algeria too, where such debates are increasingly likely to emerge, especially if Islamists should come to power. The deep ideological aspects of the FLN during the Algerian revolution, including "Third-Worldism," and the themes of Franz Fanon about the "wretched of the earth"—directly translated into the Islamic vocabulary as *mustadh'afin*—is part of a historical legacy that affects Algerian Islamist movements as well, even if more pragmatic views should dominate.

Chapter Six

HYPOTHESES ON THE FIS IN POWER: FOREIGN POLICY

As in the preceding chapter on potential FIS domestic policies in the future, any discussion of a future FIS foreign policy must be highly speculative. The following analysis and suggested hypotheses are based on a mixture of FIS statements, examination of other Islamist governments, analysis of the general dynamic of Islamist movements in general, the political culture of Algeria, and assessment of the types of problems that may arise in the future. These are only speculative hypotheses, offered to spark further examination of these issues and hopefully to provide some framework for viewing a future that cannot be known now.

THE FIS AND THE WEST

The FIS, as other Islamist organizations in North Africa, claims it has no specific anti-Western agenda, and that the West should not fear its coming to power. It states that it does not threaten Western interests and fully intends to sell gas and oil and maintain ties in the commercial and economic sphere; how Algeria tends to its domestic policies should not be of direct concern to the West. Yet this simplistic formulation is not especially reassuring to the West, since it evades all kinds of issues about the future role of the Algerian state in the international community.

There is no question that implicit within FIS thinking is a sense of cultural gap between Western and Islamic civilization. In nearly all Islamist thinking there is the sense that the West has lost its way. The quarrel is not with Christianity—although Christian culture historically has made repeated war against Islam and served as an ideology for Western colonialism against Muslim peoples. The more common accusation at the root of most Islamist thought is rather that the West has abandoned the moral precepts of Christianity itself. Islamists say they embrace modernization in its technological and educational sense, but seek to avoid the Western pattern of modernization that they perceive to be based on radical secularism, relativity of values leading to moral confusion and decline, deterioration of society, crime, juvenile problems, divorce, sexual deviancy, illegitimate children, and ultimately loss of moral direction and purpose in a celebration of the cult of individual expression regardless of social cost. As we noted earlier, the Islamists also take a strong position against the superior power and dominance of the West in the international system, especially when it comes to imposition of that power in the Middle East.

While the Islamists may have good reason to wish to avoid the mistakes, failures, and shortcomings of much of modern Western society, their own sense of the ideal society also lacks realism. While perhaps quite perspicacious about the failings of most regimes in the Middle East, the Islamists have generally failed to come up with their own clear answers and policies to pressingly urgent political, economic, and social problems. Thus, the Islamists tend to contrast the failings of Western and Middle Eastern societies against their own abstract ideal. When given the opportunity, Islamists have conspicuously failed to provide alternative governance (at least in Iran and Sudan) that demonstrates a better path to solutions of genuine and complex problems. The FIS has not developed concrete programs that suggest a major breakthrough in the practical problems of statecraft—although the possibility of effective FIS rule cannot be ruled out a priori.

Despite frequent references by the Islamists to the Qur'an and the Shari'a as central to policy, it would nonetheless be a mistake to judge the future of FIS policies based on texts or scripture alone. We should indeed pay close attention to the ways Islamists perceive the world, but in the end, Islamists are still required to live within the realm of reality and the dynamics—positive and negative—of modernization, whether it is philosophically congenial to them or not. In the end the question is not what "Islam" says (itself subject to immensely different interpretations) but what *Muslims want to do.* There is of course a danger in dismissing ideological statements in advance, since we ignore statements of intent at our peril. Nonetheless, the diversity among Islamists makes dependency upon any specific text or statement an unreliable guide to prediction of future conduct and policies.

THE FIS AND THE GULF WAR AGAINST IRAQ

The Gulf War to expel Saddam Hussain from Kuwait reveals several aspects of FIS philosophy and operational style. First, the FIS has always maintained good relations with Saudi Arabia; this is in spite of the fact that in the eyes of most Islamist movements, the Saudi regime is not Islamist at all, but corrupt, a monarchical form of government (which by definition is non-Islamic), and a traitor to the Muslim cause by virtue of its close alliance with the United States and perceived domination by U.S. policies. The FIS has long benefited from Saudi assistance and has longstanding ties with other Islamist movements in the Gulf. The FIS has always detested the Ba'th party as well, which it perceives as quintessentially secular and harsh in its oppressive treatment of Islamist activists in both Iraq and Syria. Thus, when the war began, the FIS had no reason to support Saddam Hussain at all. The radical FIS number two 'Ali Belhaj mocked Saddam in public. The first insight, then, is that this Islamist organization had some basic—atypical for Islamists—sympathies for Kuwait's plight; the policies of Saudi Arabia and other Gulf states were seemingly significant in determining the initial FIS approach to the Gulf War.

Algerian public opinion generally opposed Saddam's invasion when it first took place, and the FLN government also quickly condemned it. In Algerian eyes, however, as in so many other countries of the Muslim world, the cure to the Gulf crisis—Western military intervention from holy soil in Saudi Arabia and the prolonged, destructive siege of Iraq—was far worse than the disease of Saddam's invasion itself. Western intervention was similarly seen as preempting the possibility of the region reaching an "Arab solution" on its own to the problem. The beginnings of a vast Western armada accumulating in Saudi Arabia quickly turned the tide of public opinion in Algeria and elsewhere against the West. The masses grew highly sympathetic to

Saddam, seeing him in abstract, symbolic terms as a pillar of Arab strength and courage willing to stand up against the towering power of Western states that have imposed their will upon Arabs over so many centuries. Kuwait was viewed as rich, arrogant, and selfish, and quickly lost any sympathy as the victim of Iraqi attack.

Iraq itself thus soon came to be viewed as the victim of the West, particularly as force against Saddam escalated. Indeed, some Algerian volunteer recruits went to Jordan to prepare to support Iraq. The FIS, including its more radical wing, was gradually forced to retreat from its earlier public negative comments on Saddam to a more neutral posture that sought to mediate and finally—in light of increasing popular anger—to abandon its earlier position and to embrace a fully pro-Iraqi position. The FIS, torn between principle and practical politics, ultimately chose expediency, but the transition in its thinking took nearly two months to complete; in the end the FIS followed, rather than led, radical public opinion.[1]

What broader conclusions can be drawn from this incident? First, that FIS can be much less ideological and more expedient than anticipated. Second, the political culture of Algeria continues to express a radicalism based on its historical experience quite independent of any Islamist thinking. Third, it is difficult to discern clear-cut differences between many Islamist parties in the Arab world and many standard "Arab nationalist" positions as developed over the years. Nothing in the FIS's behavior during the Gulf War would put it sharply out of phase with most other reactions in the Arab world— nearly all of which were basically unsympathetic to Kuwait and sympathetic to Iraq as the underdog in confrontation with traditional overwhelming Western armed might.

This one incident—albeit very important and revealing—cannot, of course, offer definitive insight into FIS regional policy in the future. It would suggest, however, that the FIS will tend to reflect many of the classic Arab nationalist positions rather than some uniquely "Islamist" position. FIS policy positions will naturally vary with the issue.

---

[1] For an excellent account of the politics of the Gulf War in Algeria, from which much of these paragraphs are drawn, see Roberts (1991), pp. 131–142.

THE FIS AND ISLAMIST INTERNATIONAL POLITICS

An early concern of Western states is the likely relationship between a FIS regime and other Islamist states and movements in the world: would there arise an Islamist alliance that could then shift the balance of power in the region? Iran and Sudan, as the two Islamist states of the region so far, have both unsurprisingly expressed ideological sympathy for the FIS, and can be assumed to have lent it at least organizational advice and moral support. Indeed, both Iran and Sudan have been in regular contact with the FIS—as are almost all Islamist parties with each other. This is entirely normal. Both Iran and Sudan are rather limited in the amount of funds at their disposal (especially Sudan) for costly foreign policy initiatives, but both will try to render diplomatic and organizational assistance where possible as long as the FIS still seeks to gain power. There is no indication that any of this support, primarily political and organizational in nature—and possibly modest financial help from Iran—has had any significant impact on FIS capabilities to operate in Algeria. The FIS has drawn support far more importantly from Saudi Arabia in the past—now no longer from the state, but from private Saudi Islamists. It also has its own wealthy donors at home. It draws most of its weapons from the Algerian army itself, through raids, sympathizers, and deserters. Its guerrilla expertise comes in large measure from Algerian army officers who have abandoned the army, and from Algerians who have fought in Afghanistan. It is very difficult to make the case that radical external support has played any significant role in the position of the FIS in Algeria today. Indeed, even if the FIS were deprived of all external ties tomorrow, it is hard to imagine that the internal situation in Algeria would be any different.

A FIS in power is certain to demonstrate at least nominal solidarity with Sudan and Iran. Islamist parties and regimes have so far been generally loath to criticize each other in public, to avoid sullying the general Islamic cause. Even the FLN regime for years maintained extremely good ties with the Islamic Republic of Iran, and served as the main mediator between the United States and Iran over resolution of the hostage crisis; only under severe internal Islamist pressure in 1993—at a time when Iran continued its rhetorical support for the FIS—did Algeria finally break ties with Iran in a symbolic gesture.

Should Islamist governments multiply in the future, however, inter-relationships will almost surely change. Public fissures will predictably emerge among them, just as they do among all states of the world as the national interests of the state take precedence over ideology.[2] The FIS in power will neither require nor receive funding from either of these two states in any case, and has great gas and oil wealth of its own.

More importantly, a FIS in power almost surely will offer assistance to other Islamist movements in the region, especially in neighboring Morocco, Tunisia, and Libya. At a bare minimum this is likely to include the right of refuge to Islamist political figures in exile, and probably the right to maintain official offices and perhaps even camps within Algeria. The FIS would probably provide funding to numerous Islamist organizations as well, but would only be joining other international funders of these movements such as Saudi Arabia in the past (now mainly private funds) and the Gulf states. Assistance is most likely to go to more moderate Islamist groups that are closer to the FIS in philosophy, such as the moderate, but banned, al-Nahda movement in Tunisia, but radical personalities at the helm in the FIS would not be discriminating on issues of moderation.

The propensity of both Iran and Sudan to support aspects of international terrorism has sparked considerable Western concern in past years. That concern has probably exceeded the true dimensions of the threat to Western interests, but terrorism is always highly unsettling; its psychological impact always exceeds the material and human damage. How likely might Algeria to be to join in such activities? As we noted above, the FIS in power will probably support nearly all other Islamist organizations in the region—not necessarily the most radical and violent; but the FIS would be unlikely to distinguish between "moderate" and "violent" groups if it appeared that "two-way" terrorism, or clear-cut "state terror" against Islamists, was occurring.

---

[2]Indeed, a plethora of communist states in the world by the 1970s led to broad rivalry and conflict among them, in some cases leading to military clash and even war, especially in East Asia: the Soviet Union and China, China and Vietnam, Vietnam and Cambodia. Ideological solidarity cannot overcome clashing state interests over the passage of time.

Algerian guerrilla groups were of course very much involved in terrorism during the bloody struggle with France for independence in the 1950s and 1960s when bombings were carried out widely in France—introducing the concept of "plastique" into the common vocabulary. Algeria itself as an independent state, however, has no history of practicing international terrorism or in supporting groups that do, except for its long support for the Polisario guerrillas fighting against Morocco. Indeed, despite Algeria's strong penchant for supporting Third World activism for several decades under the FLN, Algeria has generally been businesslike in its approach to the world, has avoided involvement in radicalism, and has been sympathetic to the role of mediator between radical states and the United States, such as with Iran and Cuba in the past. While future circumstances are unpredictable, and speculation is uncertain, the FIS in power will probably not turn to international terrorism unless the state should become involved in a wholesale struggle with Western states, especially France.

Several provisos are in order. Just as the Iranian regime has pursued—and assassinated—a number of Iranian dissidents in Europe over the past decade, it is quite conceivable that the FIS in power, if engaged in a running struggle with radical and violent anti-FIS elements, might seek to pursue its enemies to Europe to dispose of them there, even as the present junta has probably done in one guise or another. Second, a serious break between France and a FIS-run Algeria could have a very negative impact on the overall situation of Muslim populations in Europe. If both sides began a spiral of provocation and if France could not come to terms with a FIS victory, leading it to undertake the destabilization of a FIS regime in Algeria, one could easily imagine the struggle being carried onto French soil, including the use of the nearly one million Algerians currently resident in France, some of whom could be recruited into terrorism. French defensive measures would undoubtedly weigh heavily on the Algerian population in France as a whole, since the entire community would fall under suspicion and the French population would demand action against Algerian terrorism. Algerian society in France would likely become highly polarized between strong secularists taking refuge in France and FIS sympathizers; conflict between the two political factions could take a violent turn within France itself.

Indeed, considerable segments of the Algerian population in France suffer economic hardship, are quite disillusioned, and feel themselves to be second-class citizens, discriminated against in social terms and made automatic objects of suspicion by the security services. The wanton public killing of a suspected Algerian terrorist created a very negative reaction among most Algerians in France, who felt that the message sent was a deliberately humiliating one, even if they had no sympathy for the Islamists.[3] The problem of Muslim integration into French society poses a major problem for all but top Algerian intellectuals and professionals. Indeed, in Europe in general, Muslim immigrants, for a variety of reasons, are not integrating successfully into society. This group could grow into a discontented separate element of society whose grievances could be open to potential exploitation, and ultimately provoke chauvinist right-wing or racist responses from local citizens.

Tensions between Algeria and France grew dramatically following the strong French support months in advance for the disputed presidential elections in Algeria in November 1995. Islamist radicals took the guerrilla war to France itself, with the hijacking of an Air France airliner and eight bombing incidents in Paris with numerous casualties. Relations between Paris and the FIS in power are likely to avoid mutual confrontations, but if Paris were to decide to try to undermine a FIS regime, further terrorist incidents in France are entirely conceivable. Hostile policies on the part of either side could become self-fulfilling prophecies for a negative spiral of deteriorating relations. Such a confrontation would represent a new phase in a confrontational drama of "Islam versus the West" in Europe; it would likely have repercussions among Muslim populations across Europe as they in turn grew increasingly fearful for their own status and their stake in European society. Even if these potentially darker scenarios (hopefully) do not materialize, there is every good reason to expect a FIS government to continue close ties with Islamist states and perhaps to work to represent their interests in dialog with the West—in full keeping with the activist tradition of Algerian foreign policy even

---

[3]"They shot him dead, and then while he was lying there on the street they kicked him like a dog and broadcast it over and over again on national television," said one observer. See Craig R. Whitney, "Muslims Angered in France; Protest the Killing of Terror Suspect," *The New York Times*, October 7, 1995.

before the FIS. Algeria might especially seek to improve U.S.-Iranian ties. But Algeria under the FIS could also develop pretensions of assuming some kind of broader international leadership of Islamist movements, perhaps even as a rival with Iran. Algeria's penchant for activism in foreign policy—especially Third World affairs—should not be overlooked when thinking about the future of the FIS.

ALGERIA AND AFRICA

Another important legacy of the FLN period was Algeria's close involvement with, and support for, radical movements in Black Africa, especially in the Congo, Mozambique, and South Africa, at least in the early years.[4] The FIS could restore attention to the Black African region, but with special focus on the Muslim states. Sudan has been active in trying to extend Islamist influence in Black Africa; the FIS may well be interested in doing the same, especially in West Africa in the Sahel countries, where resurgent Islamist movements already exist—of interest to both Iran and Sudan. Of the 45 states of sub-Saharan Africa, most have significant Muslim communities, and perhaps one-third or more—including the giant Nigeria—may have a Muslim majority.[5] Islam in Africa in general has been more closely linked with Sufi (spiritual, mystic) traditions that are often distasteful to more orthodox Islamists, since they see such movements as less-than-pure Islam. Islamists may thus readily feel a sense of mission to organize, "purify," and indeed further politicize such existing movements. It is in these regions that Algerian competition with an already activist Iranian program of contacts, preaching, and organizing could most likely emerge.

Competition rather than coordination of activities would seem, over time, to be the more likely trend, especially given the Shi'i-Sunni division between Iran and Algeria and the issues of rival state influence in Africa. Other states such as Libya and Saudi Arabia have also spread largesse in the region for the sake of their particular state and ideological interests. Cooperation at some level, especially initially, should not be ruled out. Islamist politics can only be a further

---

[4]Ruedy, p. 212.

[5]Michael Radu, "Islam and Politics in Black Africa," *Dissent,* Summer 1992, p. 408.

complicating factor in what is already a trend toward growing tribalism and separatism in Africa over the longer run:

> African Islam has recently lost many of its historic traditions of political adaptability, relative tolerance, and flexibility in favor of a variety of largely exogenous fundamentalist approaches. These serve to exacerbate the deep-rooted problems Africa has inherited since independence. African Islam, which was previously an important element in nation-building efforts and an essential factor in the self-definition of many African states, is—at least in many of its recently politicized forms—threatening now to become an obstacle to both. Increasingly manipulated from outside, reactionary in its political, economic, and social, as well as ethnic and racial attitudes, African Islam is now in danger of becoming part of the problem rather than of the solution.[6]

ALGERIA AND ITS NEIGHBORS

The greater threat to neighboring regimes comes not just from potential funding from neighboring Islamist organizations (legal or illegal) but from the "bandwagon effect" of an Islamist victory in a major Arab state. Islamists everywhere will be heartened by the event of a FIS victory in Algeria, providing their movements with new élan and a growing sense of the "inevitability" of Islamist regimes in most Arab states. A FIS victory will be similarly viewed by existing regimes as a major threat—by its very existence rather than its potential subversive activities against neighbors.

How much of an actual threat would this represent to Algeria's neighbors? Its impact will vary from state to state and will depend on internal circumstances and developments in each state. FIS circles are likely to be divided, too, on the question of "export of the revolution," as has been the case in Iran and Sudan. The more radical, internationalist group represented by 'Ali Belhaj is inclined to support external organizations, while 'Abbasi Madani is more inclined to focus on the internal scene for the consolidation of power and the implementation of programs.

---

[6]Radu, p. 413.

Egypt's regime is particularly threatened by the bandwagon effect because of its own ineffectual responses to the Islamist movement in the country. In a policy of declaring increasing hostility to the entire spectrum of the Islamist movement, and by earlier repression and marginalization of most other opposition forces, the Egyptian government is inadvertently allowing the Islamists to emerge as the sole legitimate opposition force in the country. The Egyptian situation resembles the Algerian one in the same problems of large population, massive urban sprawl, limited housing, high unemployment, ineffective social services, and widely perceived corruption. The regime in Egypt, too, has been unwilling to engage in dialog or a tactic of "inclusion" of Islamist forces—even moderate, nonviolent ones. The government is also making the mistake of offering the people virtually no choice between the stark alternatives of the regime versus the Islamists ("if you don't like me, see how you like the Islamists"). Violence between the regime and the Islamists in Egypt is at the highest level anywhere in the Muslim world outside of Algeria.

While a majority of Egyptians might not yet choose the Islamists over the regime—especially in a state that has lacked a radical populist revolutionary tradition—the choice may lead many to quietly abandon the government, leaving it increasingly "hollowed out" and susceptible to destabilizing mass protests down the road. While many conditions—social, geographic, historical, cultural—differ considerably between Egypt and Algeria, the similarities of the predicament over time are growing. The coming to power of the FIS will undoubtedly greatly stimulate and enhance the psychological position of the Islamists in Egypt. Egypt will see itself as the leader of counter-Islamist forces in the region. Egypt's newfound interest in joining the Arab-Maghreb Union in October 1994 in part reflects a concern for the growing importance of North Africa to the Islamist movement. Egypt is very likely already providing the current Algerian regime advice, expertise, training, and intelligence on how to handle the Islamist challenge, even though the characters of the two states differ considerably.

If the FIS comes to power in Algeria, it is quite possible that the FIS and Cairo will view each other as sworn enemies. Under those circumstances, Algeria could cooperate with Sudan in an effort to further support the Islamist movement in Egypt. But Egyptian Islamists do not require Algerian assistance for the prospering of their own cause, and it would probably make little difference on the ground. Alternatively, the FIS could attempt to "take a higher road" and work to persuade Cairo to let it serve as a mediator in the internal Egyptian conflict; Cairo would not take kindly to such offers, however. Cairo may take the lead to organize the other states of the Maghreb against a FIS challenge from Algeria.

In neighboring Morocco, King Hassan has been one of the most successful Arab rulers in dominating Morocco's own Islamist movements, for a variety of reasons: his greater legitimacy, blood ties to the Prophet, a more successful and diversified economy, and a shrewder handling of Islamist and other parties.[7] Indeed, Morocco reportedly has received FIS members in the country, and, according to one account, the king has even received them personally, much to the anger of the Algerian regime.[8] The king might thus be partly insured if change were to come in Algeria. Deteriorating economic and social conditions in Morocco of course do tend to work to the benefit of the Islamist challengers.

But Algeria has generally had poor relations with Morocco over the past several decades. The two states have totally different political experiences. Both are rivals for regional leadership. The rivalry is likely to continue into a period of FIS rule, despite King Hassan's efforts to maintain ties with the FIS. The question of the West Sahara and lingering border issues will probably fuel the friction. Algeria has supported the nominal independence of a "Sahrawi (Saharan) Arab Democratic Republic"—in reality not a state but a guerrilla movement led by the Polisario Front—on land that Morocco sees as inseparably part of its own territory. The Saharan conflict has continued for nearly two decades; an eventual UN-sponsored referendum is to decide the fate of the region. The issue is still burning and could well cause conflict between Algeria and Morocco if Algeria provides further military assistance to the Polisario Front. Unresolved border issues, involving Moroccan claims to Algerian territory taken in the last century under French administration by military force, further

---

[7]For a discussion of Maghreb-wide Islamist politics, see, for example, Leveau, *Le Sabre et le Turban*, and Burgat, *The Islamic Movement in North Africa*.

[8]See Soudan, p. 12.

complicate the issue. While neither of these issues must inevitably lead to conflict, they provide the wherewithal for conflict that could be stimulated as well by regional rivalry, ideological differences, or outspoken FIS support for Islamist activist groups in Morocco and the provision of a safe haven to banned leaders.

Tunisia might fare less well under ideological pressure than Morocco. This is not the place to analyze Tunisian politics and the role of the Islamists in it; it is worth noting that Tunisia has been an intellectual center for nationalist and religious leadership from Algeria during much of this century. Rashid Ghannushi, the Tunisian Islamist leader of al-Nahda now in exile in London—and considered a moderate among Islamists—is in close touch with the FIS.[9] The demonstration effect of a FIS victory in Algeria would have great, but not necessarily decisive, impact on Tunisia, since the Tunisian regime has fairly tight control over its Islamists. The Tunisian regime in any case has opted for repression over accommodation at this point, believing that an expected upturn in the economy within a few years ("light at the end of the economic tunnel") will then improve social conditions, rendering the Islamists then politically irrelevant, at which time democracy can be restored. In the author's view, the rationale is open to question, but Tunisia is a small, manageable society whose economy may help the regime pull through the period of its greatest vulnerability to Islamism.

Libya is also susceptible to a great increase in Islamist influence in the future. While the Libyan situation differs sharply from the Algerian or Egyptian—small population, little desperate urban poverty—the Islamists are again the only significant functioning opposition force. All Islamists have the advantage of being able to work from within mosque structures with ready access thereby to the public, something other political parties are harder put to organize. The country also has a long-standing tradition of Islamic activism in politics going back to the monarchy.

---

[9]Shaykh Ghannushi, in an interview with the author in London in October 1994, points out that his own organization is more moderate than the FIS: whereas his al-Nahda party derives its support primarily from the middle class, the FIS, in Ghannushi's view, draws its support more from the dispossessed, and thus is inclined to a greater radicalism. In any case, Ghannushi claims, the Islamist movement in the Middle East today is not about Islam versus secularism or Islam versus the West so much as about "peoples versus the rulers" *(al-shu'ub didh al-hukkam)*.

OIL POLICIES

Based on the history of radical regimes and oil sales and production in the Middle East, it is extremely unlikely that the FIS in power would cut off gas and oil production to the West. The state will desperately require heavy revenues to implement ambitious social programs; revenues will be a new regime's first agenda. No radical leader has ever cut off oil flow to the West in the past—not Qadhafi, not Saddam Hussain, and not the Ayatollah Khomeini. If any leaders have thought of using the "oil weapon" against the West, it has been King Faysal of Saudi Arabia in 1973, with the oil boycott against the United States, and talk by the Shah of Iran about the need to raise the price of oil dramatically in view of its importance as a "noble element."

Thus, few immediate reasons can be anticipated for any kind of gas-cutoff policy—indeed, none has so far arisen with Algeria over any regional issue, including close U.S. support for Morocco and its staunch support of Israel. Algeria under the FIS may nonetheless be likely to push for higher energy prices. This position is consistent with its foreign policy of over 25 years that emphasized a fairer deal for commodity-producing Third World nations, and with Algeria's championing of a New World Economic Order proclaimed at the UN in 1974 as part of the agenda of the Third World Group of 77 in which Algeria took a leading role. Indeed, this predisposition may well be a growing trend in the post–Cold War world in any case, as many countries struggle within the international economic order, the rigors of IMF reform guidelines, and the tribulations of the marketization process, coupled with their own mismanagement and overpopulation. Even if Algeria has grown more pragmatic and less "Third World" in its outlook in the last decade, the intellectual roots are still present and cannot be dismissed. The FIS might marginally strengthen that approach, depending on the degree of radicalism its ultimate leadership will possess.

FIS RELATIONS WITH THE UNITED STATES

Several negative as well as positive determinants exist that will affect the future of a FIS-ruled Algeria and its relations with the United States. On balance, one may be guardedly optimistic.

On the negative side, Algeria has a history of portraying the United States over the years as the leader of the imperialist camp and dominating the world order. The United States has also taken the lead over the years in "disciplining" the Middle East, with military interventions against Lebanon, Syria, Iraq, Iran, and Libya. The United States has also taken a tough line with both Iran and Sudan as Islamist states and the "struggle against terrorism." It has almost consistently supported Israel in the Middle East against other states.

On the positive side, however, the United States was the first Western country to recognize Algeria's independence. It has never had direct clashes with Algeria, despite consistent disagreements over Third World policy issues. The United States has no colonial baggage in Algeria, unlike France. English is growing in popularity as a culturally "neutral" language in Algeria's linguistic "culture wars." U.S. declaratory policy in recent years on Islam has been positively received in the region, including by Islamists, particularly to the effect that the United States has no problem with Islam per se, but that it opposes radicalism of any kind and origin, and that it supports democracy and human rights. The Islamists read this latter point as objectively in their interests since they are among the foremost victims of state oppression and regularly denied access to a democratic order.

But Islamists accuse the United States of applying a double standard in its unwillingness to speak out more forcefully against human rights violations against Islamists in friendly countries. The FIS has noted that the United States has publicly stated that it does not believe a military solution can solve the present conflict in Algeria and that all parties to the conflict need to talk. The FIS does not believe that the United States is specifically hostile—even if Washington is nervous about future FIS policies and behavior. The FIS also notes that U.S. policies have been far more liberal and tolerant toward the FIS than French policies have been. Many Islamists in the Middle East sometimes comment that Americans are "more open" than Europeans, seem to have fewer hang-ups about the Third World and Islam. Strikingly, as we have noted, no American citizens have been killed by Algerian terrorists to date, although some of that is due to a relatively small American official and commercial presence. On balance then, Algeria under the FIS could start out relatively well disposed toward the United States.

At least two issues exist that can negatively affect U.S. relations with Algeria under the FIS. The first is terrorism, discussed above. If Algeria should become the seat of a new movement for the export of the revolution, in ways deeply destabilizing to the region, relations with Washington will quickly deteriorate. Today, as the situation in Algeria itself continues to deteriorate, the rate of terrorism is in fact rising, particularly as directed against foreigners, even foreign diplomats and even exported to France. The GIA is seemingly the chief perpetrator of these threats and acts. The first critical question then becomes the degree of meaningful distinction between the GIA and the FIS. Are these simply two factions of a single organization that have agreed to disagree and coexist, a form of the "good cop, bad cop" game—politically meaningless in its impact on the outside world? Or does it represent a true, serious, deep division that the FIS would be expected to handle in the event of a political victory? If FIS-GIA differences are real and profound—and of vital concern to the FIS itself—then it will be critical for the FIS to be able to articulate those differences now. It will need to convince the electorate that it can and will attend to the problems of extremism among other Islamists that ultimately threaten *any* state order.[10]

The second issue is Algerian intentions on proliferation of nuclear weapons. Algeria, as the second-biggest state in Africa after Sudan, views itself as a natural leader of the region. An Algerian official privately commented that in the 21st century there will be two superpowers in Africa, South Africa and Algeria, and that it would not be surprising if both sought to strengthen this status with nuclear weapons. The FIS will be heir to all the FLN's regional ambitions and will probably add a few of its own, particularly relating to increasing the power of the Islamic world. A determined effort by Algeria to acquire nuclear weapons would lead to strong U.S. resistance, fully supported by France.

The United States could also become involved in Algerian affairs if a FIS in power leads to internal purges, chaos, and potential civil war. While the French would have the lead responsibility in handling

---

[10]This problem resembles the very complex difficulty of the PLO and its handling of the radical Islamist "Islamic Jihad" organization; is the PLO itself better poised to handle this problem of Islamist violence, or is it the Israelis, as the enemy and with even tougher methods?

refugee problems, the United States as part of a broader NATO response could eventually take part in peacekeeping operations or efforts to keep the conflict from spreading outside Algeria.

If the FIS adopted a strong, destabilizing policy toward either Tunisia or Morocco, especially the latter, the United States, perhaps with NATO partners, could also be drawn in. If the southern Sahara conflict were to worsen, or lead to military clashes between Morocco and Algeria designed to stir up chaos in Morocco, Washington could well end up assisting Morocco with military aid and support against Algeria. The same could be true with military challenges to Tunisia—but is less likely. This is not to say that the United States will support either of those states automatically against a FIS-ruled Algeria, but if the FIS were undermining them as part of a clear and deliberate policy, U.S.—and European—interests would be directly affected.

U.S. private-sector investment in Algeria is highly significant and will be a constant ameliorating factor in bilateral U.S.-Algerian relations. Despite the bad social and economic conditions of Algeria today, its economic problems are mainly political, stemming from mismanagement. With the rich energy resources of the country, Algeria could have a bright future if it can manage its complex process of development and growth into a politically mature nation.

*   *   *

This sketch of potential FIS policies in power is written under the assumption that the FIS will have broad control of the reins of government and will be relatively free to apply such policies as it desires. In reality, however, the FIS will not necessarily gain absolute control over national policy. In any scenario of power sharing with other forces via a "nondemocratic deal," or by election victory in which it operates under normal, legal constitutional constraints, the FIS will be constrained in its policy options and less likely to pursue a radical course. Thus, these speculations based on behavior and ideology will inevitably be tempered by the realities of the situation.

Chapter Seven

THE STRUGGLE FOR POWER: CONFRONTATION OR RECONCILIATION?

THE FIS AND THE ARMY

The army and the FIS stand at opposite ends of the political spectrum at present. It is "the army" that most strongly opposes the FIS's coming to power. But two important points need to be made in this respect. First, the army is not uniform in its outlook, and it reflects something of the ideological and regional divisions of the FLN itself. It is valuable to look at what the army in fact represents within the Algerian state and society. In particular, there is within the army a strong resentment of the failure of FLN stewardship over the country in the past decade—with which the army has been intimately linked. In the eyes of one key French scholar on the Maghreb,

> the corporatist interests of the officers, their desire to preserve their independence and the necessary resources for the military's functioning, their feeling of distance from a political clique [FLN] that is tainted by corruption, divided and timid—these are the key elements that characterize the relationship of the military to the workings of state institutions that have been so long associated now with the image of authoritarian power.[1]

Indeed, the comment has been made that Algeria is really "an army that has a state," so deeply has the army been associated with FLN

---

[1] Leveau (1993), pp. 205–206.

rule.[2] The military has often been brought in by failing state policies to crush popular uprisings, and it no longer wishes to have to play this police role. Here lies the essence of the question of military loyalty to junta anti-FIS policy in the future.

The source of much hard-line anti-FIS sentiment stems mostly from the older elements of the army. The Algerian army still contains many recruits from the days of the French army, especially after the heavy recruiting during World War II to meet the German onslaught in Europe, and later in Vietnam. But these close cultural ties with France maintained by the officers of the preindependence Algerian army in no way suggest any kind of political dependence upon France today. In fact, it was the break with France during the liberation struggle that gave the Algerian army its defining character. Nonetheless, the political culture of the army remains heavily imbued by the French experience and French professional training—and a French secular outlook to a considerable extent. The Algerian army today thus presents a fascinating ambivalence: in many ways it is one of the more francophone elements among the population, yet its patriotism and commitment to the Algerian nation is powerful and unquestioned, despite the weak use of Arabic within its ranks.[3]

The army also reflects differences among three types of officer: those who belong to the old struggle for national liberation, those who fought in the old French-created Algerian army, and those educated in the modern Middle East. Former presidents Boumedienne and Benjadid have both known how to skillfully play off these diverse factions against each other. Those who stem from the old liberation struggle are today perceived as the most reactionary and least inclined to accept sweeping reforms, even within the FLN and the state structure.[4] Indeed, when reformist president Muhammad Boudiaf was assassinated in 1993, it was widely suspected that it was not the FIS behind the killing, but French-oriented officers who aimed to stop the purge of the FLN and the army.[5] This group today is con-

---

[2]Mileb, p. 14.

[3]Leveau (1993), pp. 210–212.

[4]Leveau (1993), p. 212.

[5]"Librahimi: These are the Murderers of President Boudiaf," *Mideast Mirror*, April 27, 1994.

temptuously referred to by the FIS as the "French party" *(hizb fransa).*

Finally, there are also regional interests reflected within the army that could, in the event of widespread civil war within the country, become regional warlords conducting their own military policy in the absence of any strong functioning center. FLN leadership in the past has also balanced among these contending regional interests in the army.

Yet today there are also younger officers who are not part of the old spoils system of the army and have little to lose in a purge and reform of an institution that is widely perceived as corrupted and tainted through its long and intimate association with FLN rule. It is quite possible that many younger officers may well defect to the FIS in view of the seeming inflexibility and unreformability of the army.[6] Under these circumstances, one could even imagine a civil war in which different elements of the army fight on different sides.

The FIS, furthermore, has unquestionably sought to infiltrate the military—as Islamist and other ideological groups have done elsewhere in the Middle East. Indeed, the Islamist "ultra-secret Da'wa Organization" (not the same as the Da'wa League of the prestigious Shaykh Sahnun) has set itself the specific goal of infiltrating the army in order to gain supporters, and is formally part of the FIS.[7] It is interesting to note that the National Islamic Front in Sudan was able to come to power in 1979, via a military coup, specifically because of patient building of sympathetic cadres within the military over many years; this included the opportunity to legally provide the military with training in Islamic principles at the behest of the state as an antidote to communist influence.

Today, it is impossible for any external observer to gauge the degree of Islamist infiltration into the Algerian army; indeed, the Algerian regime itself probably cannot be sure. The logic of events—and parallels with other states such as Egypt, where radical Islamists created cells within the Egyptian army, enabling them to assassinate President Sadat—suggests then that we will learn of the true degree

---

[6]Mileb, p. 16.

[7]Yared (1992), p. 47.

of pro-Islamist sentiment within the Algerian military only after the breakdown of the current ruling junta or actual FIS attainment of power.

Perhaps even the public emergence of a pro-FIS element within the army cannot be excluded in the near future. Such a group might demand that the regime open up negotiations with the FIS in order to bring civil conflict to an end. While the top leadership of the military is today militantly determined to keep the FIS out at all costs, it appears to be increasingly losing touch with reality; compromise does not seem to be part of its vocabulary, even while it lacks a coherent plan for changing the situation other than "toughing it out." Continuing crisis, however, may eventually cause this echelon of the military to be superseded by lower-ranking officers with a better grasp of the deterioration of the country under the present conditions.

The grip of the military on the FLN and the state actually began to be broken with the reform process within the FLN itself in the late 1980s. At the historic FLN congress in November 1989, the army pulled out of the ruling coalition—perhaps seeing the FLN already in a state of fatal decline and wishing to avoid being dragged down with it. In fact, in the early days of President Chadli's reformist policies, the army seemed to take a liberal position on granting concessions to the FIS. It was only after the FIS began to take the political struggle to the streets in broad rioting that the army supported a harsh crackdown against it. In short, the army at that time was willing to go along with elections, but not with a breakdown of law and order.[8] Today the top level of the military is unlikely to even contemplate elections that would permit the FIS to openly contest the junta for political power.

Army officers, like so many other secularized elements within society, had also grown nervous about the social implications of FIS social policy; many of their wives were schoolteachers and first-hand witnesses of the slow hand of social repression as the Islamists gained dominance in much of the educational field; they wanted their wives to continue to earn a livelihood and to have the freedom

---

[8]Mortimer, p. 590.

to walk the streets, go the university, or go to the beach. Officers were also concerned that a FIS regime would cut off the ties of French language, books, and journals with Europe, which would lead to the isolation of Algerian culture and technology.[9]

THE FIS, "FILS" OF THE FLN?

On the one hand, then, army hostility toward the FIS stems from the military's ties with French culture, language, training, operational philosophy, and a profoundly modernist, secularist outlook—the dominant strains of an anti-FIS outlook. But this is only half the story. On the other hand, there is an ambivalence toward the FIS that flows out of the same Algerian culture. The army shares with the FIS a deeper strain of xenophobia toward the West, reflecting in part traditional Arab nationalism and in part the unique trauma of the liberation struggle that Algeria fought alone—without even moral support from a West that is supposed to champion self-determination of peoples. This jaundiced view of Western intentions thoroughly permeates both the army and the FLN itself, imbuing the army with a de facto commonality of view with the FIS on aspects of the Western threat. Surprisingly—and in an exceptionally paranoid vein—the army was suspicious of FIS ties with Islamist circles in the Gulf because it saw such Gulf ties as de facto linked with the United States; the fear was that the United States actually supported the FIS coming to power—via Gulf state influence—with the express aim of weakening Algeria so as the better to dominate it.

The FIS and the army also shared many outlooks on the Gulf War: while very Arab nationalist in outlook, the army viewed Saddam Hussain as a fool to be blind to the military and technical power of the Western military machine. The FIS, too, as we have seen, was originally deeply suspicious of Saddam Hussain and his Ba'thi secularist principles, and came to support Saddam only because of pressures from the street.[10] The FIS ultimately shares then with the army a suspicion and distrust of Western intentions that they perceive as aimed at the emasculation of Algerian power. There is no doubt in

---

[9]Leveau (1993), p. 218.

[10]Ibid., p. 219.

army circles that FIS shares this heritage. "A common theme of opposition to the West would bring [the FIS] closer to the army."[11] These common themes run deeper yet, embracing simplistic views of some kind of Anglo-Gallic struggle for power over the soul of Algeria:

> Public anti-French rhetoric is part of the style adopted by all parties in Algerian political life and the FIS hardly indulges in it any more than the FLN. Should any credence be given [then] to the theories among the Algerian military and politicians on the role the FIS might play in introducing American influence into the Maghreb, via the Saudis and the system of Islamic banks?[12]

In this respect, too, then, the FIS, the army, and the FLN all share certain elements of a common culture that renders the apparent polarization of views and interests between these two groups far less sharp than one might assume in the West.

AN ARMY-FIS RESOLUTION?

We have examined some of the striking similarities between the FIS and the FLN on a variety of issues. Both share an intensely nationalist outlook, especially the "Algerianist" wing of the FIS as opposed to its much smaller "internationalist" wing. Both FIS and FLN share a xenophobia toward the outside world, not always identical in all respects, but mutually reinforcing. Both believe deeply in preservation of the integrity of Algerian culture, which for both groups includes Islam. Many in the army share the view that the FLN has become hopelessly corrupted and out of touch with the masses and with reality. Both have a somewhat utilitarian view of democracy and liberalization: the army and the FIS attach far higher priority to the attainment of other national goals than to the lower priority of political liberalization of the country per se, but both recognize that under certain circumstances democracy could play a useful role. Both could probably dispense with democratic procedure if need be, and they perhaps could even cooperate in this regard. These commonalities suggest, then, that the two institutions share something of a

---

[11]Remy Leveau, *Algeria: Adversaries in Search of Uncertain Compromises*, Paris: Institute for Security Studies, Western European Union, September 1992.

[12]Ibid., p. 17.

common outlook on key political and cultural problems of Algerian society. In the eyes of many, FIS is almost trying to "do better" what the FLN set out to do in the first place, but failed.

But there are differences as well that have more to do with sharing power than with ideology. The army is determined to maintain its independence as the premier national institution. It will not permit itself—if possible—to be taken over by the FIS. (Nonetheless, the army did permit itself to be "taken over" by the FLN to a considerable extent, and only in 1989 decided to formally break away simply because it did not wish to be dragged down by FLN's deterioration.) The army likewise apologizes to no one for its francophone orientation in a culture more broadly focused on Arabization (under either FLN or FIS direction). The army is also deeply secular in its vision of lifestyle—perhaps its single significant ideological difference with FIS. The senior command of the military is also determined that it alone will handle the struggle against the FIS without having to resort to the creation of local militias, which it sees as a source of decentralization of military power and potential increase of civil conflict among local factions.[13]

Thus, a great deal of the clash between the two institutions has to do with power. The FIS basically challenges the entire status quo of the Algerian experience. It challenges the corruption of the system—in which the army has been a basic participant. If the old state structure is weakened or decapitated, the army could also be a victim of the process—precisely the position of the old guard in the military, and in the FLN as well. The army could, however, eventually choose to seriously distance itself from this political process, in order to salvage its independence and autonomy within the system. The less the army is used as a national police institution to kill other Algerians, the "purer" it will be in its independent role within the state. For the military, therefore, the current struggle is a critical one. If the army decides to defend the old order—whose only real challenger at the popular level is the FIS—then its independence is compromised and it will pay the price if the FIS comes to power. If the army is independent, there is no reason why the old ruling combination of state,

---

[13]See Paul-Marie De La Gorce, "Voyage au coeur de l'armee," *Jeune Afrique*, April 21, 1994, p. 21.

army, and FLN could not be transformed into the state, army, and FIS.

Despite the violent and uncompromising struggle between the army and the FIS today, there has nonetheless been a series of nominal efforts by the regime to "negotiate" with the opposition, including the FIS. The press has reported on a number of contacts between the regime and the FIS jailed leadership in a supposed effort to find some compromise. These talks have usually been broken off by the regime, charging the FIS with bad faith and unwillingness to compromise. FIS leaders have charged that the contacts were purely charades, designed to increase the regime's extremely narrow domestic support and to placate Algeria's foreign critics who have called for a political dialog. In any case, given the distance between the positions of the two camps, it is not surprising that regime-FIS negotiations have gone nowhere.

There is simply no way that the junta will ever seem ready to permit a situation to develop whereby the FIS would have even a chance of coming to power—even by democratic means. Similarly, as long as the FIS will compromise only on how to gain access to power, the junta will not negotiate and the standoff will continue. But eventually the impasse will be broken, either by the emergence of a far broader, democratic government coalition or by the eventual collapse of regime power.

In sum, then, despite total irreconcilability of the junta and the FIS on the question of access to power, in a broader sense the FIS and the army do not have to be inexorably and inevitably on a collision course. A compromise could emerge more easily than most observers have thought, once the army either rethinks the long-term cost of its position or finds more moderate officers taking over at the top.

Along this line of thinking then, the real drama of Algeria is within the military itself—a difference between generations, between experiences, between factions, and between differing visions of "Algerianness" and its relationship to modernity. Once the military resolves this struggle within its own ranks, it must then commit itself to an independent course of action to break the deadlock. An eventual compromise between the military and the FIS is thus conceivable—

despite the hard, uncompromising lines drawn today. Compromise could come along one of two lines, democratic or nondemocratic .

THE NONDEMOCRATIC COMPROMISE

A compromise between the military and the FIS on a nondemocratic level would involve a negotiated agreement whereby the FIS accepted an agreed-upon proportion of power—such as appointment of a FIS prime minister and several cabinet ministers, accompanied by an agreed-upon proportion of seats in the parliament. This kind of agreement would put an end to further rivalry for power—at least for the interim. Utilizing the power today to appoint a FIS prime minister would also be virtually the only way the army could guarantee itself a formal voice in a new regime not otherwise legitimated by elections. Such an arrangement in effect would *anticipate and preempt elections* by recognizing the inevitability of FIS accession to power at least by a plurality in an election—but would spare the country the trauma of what would undoubtedly be an ugly electoral campaign.

How would the FIS respond to such "an offer they could not refuse" from the army? First of all, the FIS has officially stated that it will not accept a "Sudan-type deal" of nondemocratic accession to power— that may be accurate—at least for now. For the FIS there are clear pluses and minuses. Acceptance of a prearranged distribution of power would guarantee the FIS access to power—quickly and without the complexity and uncertainty of a long election campaign that might reveal differences among the various elements of the FIS.[14] On the other hand, if the FIS is convinced that it would prevail with at least a plurality in an election, then to compromise with the military on a prearranged power-sharing formula might give the FIS less power within the government than it might otherwise hope for via elections. It would also deprive the FIS of genuine democratic legitimacy—and would suggest that the army could also remove it from power at will, without suffering the consequences of legal violation of

---

[14]Indeed, some Algerian observers are convinced that the FIS could never afford to have a national congress, that it knows it could never reach consensus and would demonstrate to the world and to its own followers the degree to which it is deeply riven and unable to agree on concrete policies on which to campaign more effectively.

a legitimate, elected government. The FIS's dilemma could therefore be significant.

On the other hand, key elements of the FIS may consider with the passage of time and continuing civil war that it is perhaps only losing power to the ultraradicals and militants within the ranks of the Islamists. They might see the continuing violence as making the top army leadership and even the population ever more implacably hostile to the dangers of a FIS victory at the polls. Under these circumstances, then, the FIS might decide to settle for the realistic gain of real but limited power via a nondemocratic sharing of power with the military. The military too, might find this the most attractive solution from its point of view, for it would be able to control the process and be in a position to prevent the FIS from adopting too-radical policies within the state structure.

THE "SANT' EGIDIO" BREAKTHROUGH

A new variable entered the Algerian political scene with two extraordinary meetings in Rome in November 1994 and January 1995, under the aegis of the Roman Catholic peace group called the Sant' Egidio Community. Eight Algerian parties—virtually all the country's major political parties, including the FIS—met to urge a negotiated solution upon the Algerian regime.[15] The two convocations were remarkable from several points of view:

- The representation of almost all major parties reflected an exceptionally high proportion of the potential Algerian electorate— giving its peace plan a particular legitimacy unmatched by almost any other political forum in Algeria in decades.

- The FIS joined the other parties in the talks, thereby taking a significant further step in the direction of "normalization" as a party; the FIS similarly received the support of the other parties

---

[15]See *Mideast Mirror*, November 23, 1994, p. 17, and January 11, 1995, p. 23; William Drozdiak, "Algerian Parties Unite in Call for Peace Talks," *Washington Post*, January 16, 1995; Alan Riding, "Algeria's Most Radical Islamic Group Seeks Pact, with Conditions," *The New York Times*, January 16, 1995; Andrew J. Pierre and William B. Quandt, "The 'Contract' with Algeria," *Washington Post*, January 22, 1995.

not only as a legitimate, but as an indispensable part of any future political dialog with the state.

- The parties expressed the desire of their supporters for an end to violence and the search for a legitimate democratic government formed through elections.

The Sant' Egidio formula basically took Algerian politics out of the hands of the regime and arrogated self-appointed power to the political parties themselves to reach political compromise. The junta in Algiers denounced the Sant' Egidio process as an attempt to usurp government power. In effect, the challenge to the regime was great. The regime would have preferred to deal with the political parties singly, to divide them and attempt to coopt some of them. The united front set up by the parties, under the freedom of convening abroad, posed a challenge nearly as great as a call for fully open elections. The parties also hoped that the international community would support the Sant' Egidio process and compel the regime to accept it. In the event, that did not happen; while foreign governments, including Washington, had positive things to say about Sant' Egidio as indicating a means to a peaceful resolution, no foreign state moved to impose the process on Algiers.

Following the Sant' Egidio meetings and their rejection by the regime, President Liamin Zerwal announced that presidential elections would be held as a means of returning to legitimacy the political process in the country. The holding of presidential elections was nonetheless denounced by all Sant' Egidio parties as not answering the basic need—to restore free and open parliamentary elections in which all parties—including the FIS—would compete. Because the regime was inflexible on the necessity of holding presidential elections first—which the opposition parties feared would be a ruse for lending legitimacy to an illegitimate regime—they chose to boycott the elections. Nonetheless, the elections were duly held, and despite the boycott and threats of violence, an astonishingly high proportion of the electorate turned out—estimated at perhaps 75 percent of potential voters—and accorded President Zerwal 61 percent of the vote.

The presidential elections have been a subject of much controversy—appropriately, since the interpretation of their significance weighs heavily upon Algeria's political future. The elections can be viewed as establishing some degree of legitimacy to the present regime on the following grounds:

• The turnout was relatively high.

• Most observers felt that the elections were relatively honest with minimal reports of irregularities.

• The elections involved some real choice among four candidates who offered partially differing programs, including the moderate Islamist and leader of Hamas, Mahfoudh Nahnah, who was runner up with 25 percent of the vote.

• This was one of the few genuinely contested presidential elections in the Arab world.

The elections, however, can be significantly faulted in a number of respects, particularly from the opposition point of view:

• None of the three major political parties in the country was represented: not the FIS, the FLN, or the FSS.

• The election did nothing to reintroduce the role of political parties into the process.

• The elections served the (possibly undesirable) purpose of lending a partial mantle of legitimacy to a ruling junta that subverted the political process in 1992 and may not go further in legitimating the existence of a genuine opposition.

• The regime may now assume it has a domestic and international license to continue to suppress the FIS by violent means.

The true significance of the elections will be contested for some time. Most interpreters believe that the votes were really a victory for the people who are sick of violence and political illegitimacy, and who flocked to the polls to state that they want legitimacy and an end to bloodshed.[16] Despite opposition denunciation of them up to election day, it is important to note that a leading FIS spokesman in Germany, Rabih Kabir, addressed Zerwal in an open letter as "Mr.

---

[16]See, for example, Hamou Amrouche, a former Algerian government official, "The Real Significance of the Algerian Presidential Elections," *The Boston Globe*, November 26, 1995; also *Mideast Mirror*, November 23, 1995, p. 16.

President," urged him to use the "mandate" he received to bring about a national reconciliation, and called for a national dialog.[17] The FLN leader likewise congratulated Zerwal and expressed willingness to take part in any endeavor to end the national crisis. The FSS has also made conciliatory gestures toward Zerwal. These steps indicate that the three leading parties consider the elections to have been a victory for Zerwal in spite of their opposition, and that he is now the force to be dealt with.

The most critical issue in Zerwal's victory is its significance for the hard-liners in the junta. Did Zerwal win a victory for a more conciliatory policy over the hard-liners? Has he now won a mandate to move ahead with his own agenda, or has he simply gained some mantle of legitimacy to continue the same policies of the past—including the continued rejection of any serious dialog with the FIS? Only time will tell. But one interpretation of the elections could be that the junta's hard-line policies have "worked," that is, the radical and most violent have been put on the defensive, they seemingly have no prospect for their own military victory, they were unable to stop the elections and the (partial) legitimization of Zerwal's regime, and the international community has been unwilling to undercut Zerwal and in fact is willing to accord him a greater degree of legitimacy (and time) than he has had in the past. Why, then, should the regime go on to make concessions to the FIS when it is in a position to continue to marginalize it in the political process?

These questions will only be answered over time as Zerwal's future actions and policies are gradually revealed. Despite the significant tactical milestone represented by the presidential elections, the author is inclined to support a modified form of the views expressed in the last paragraph: that the regime still does not face pressure or have an incentive to deal with the FIS. According to this interpretation then, the following features will characterize the period ahead:

- Zerwal will seek to break up the unity of the Sant' Egidio grouping of opposition parties by coopting certain of them into political cooperation, most likely either the "new" FLN or the FSS.

---

[17]*Mideast Mirror,* November 24, 1995, p. 9.

- Zerwal will continue to express his formula that the regime will only deal with elements that eschew violence—a formula that on the surface is unexceptionable and would enjoy general international support. On the other hand, it is the type of formula that, shrewdly used, can serve to indefinitely exclude the FIS from any association with power, since as long as police and army violence is employed against the party, it will not agree to drop violence, especially with no guarantee that it will then be accorded legal status. The FIS, furthermore, may not be able to control radical GIA elements for some time as long as the GIA is convinced that the regime is only seeking to weaken and destroy the FIS rather than deal with it as a legitimate legal party. Indeed, Anwar Haddam, the FIS representative in Washington, denounced Rabih Kabir's conciliatory statement from Germany as "betraying" the FIS cause to a regime that still has no legitimacy.

- The unity of the Sant' Egidio group is in fact likely to break up under manipulation and cooption efforts by the regime. That will increase some degree of political bitterness if the FIS or any other major party feels it has been abandoned for opportunistic reasons.

The international community is not, of course, eager to see the Islamists enter into political power and will thus give the Zerwal regime the maximum benefit of the doubt in his assertions of interest in opening a national dialog. If a national dialog and some degree of stability can be established while sidelining the FIS, no great tears will be shed. But that is the key question: has the FIS been effectively sidelined? In the author's view, the FIS has indeed been struck a blow, both in political and military terms, but it has been far from marginalized on the political scene. It is undoubtedly true that the Algerian public is sickened by the horrific violence that has been dealt by both sides in the conflict, in which hardly anyone has been left untouched or unshaken. The particular brutality of GIA operations against leading journalists, politicians, writers, artists, and intellectuals has been particularly shocking, causing the FIS to lose much support that it might have had earlier. The FIS is furthermore in considerable disarray, given the arrest of its key leaders and their inability to meet and communicate or to formulate political positions. Thus, decentralized guerrilla units have a major voice in public perception of "what the FIS really is."

But the FIS nonetheless represents a significant segment of the population; its roots have been discussed in detail in earlier chapters. It is not likely that any other party at this point represents that constituency; the FIS simply cannot drop off the political spectrum without leaving a major vacuum. The FIS will have to invent itself anew if it is not there. The political experience of the rest of the Arab world gives further credence to the idea of the "legitimacy," cultural roots, and political incentives for such parties to emerge. But this does not mean that the FIS will necessarily always be the dominant political force either. Indeed, it is the author's basic contention that if the FIS takes a place within the political process, it will of its own accord eventually come to take on the characteristics of a "normal" minority party, gaining perhaps 10–20 percent of the vote on a regular basis. But that will not happen until the political process is regularized and the party shows what it can and cannot do for its supporters.

This study thus remains skeptical that Zerwal has gained sufficient legitimacy to preside over a national reconciliation; there furthermore remains significant doubt that forces in the army will permit a political reconciliation that will grant FIS a place on the electoral scene. In accordance with this interpretation, Islamist forces are likely to continue some kind of violence in response to the state's continued suppression of Islamists by force and violence and its unwillingness to accept the FIS. Such a scenario will essentially condemn the country to a longer period of authoritarian rule, perhaps leavened by some expansion of the government to include elements of other major parties.

An alternative scenario along more optimistic lines posits a more enlightened regime policy that leads to a shrinking of the FIS to manageable proportions before it is finally included in the political process:

- Zerwal moves to incrementally include more representatives of other political parties within the government.

- Time demonstrates a significant loss of popular FIS support as a result of prolonged violence over past years.

- The inclusion of other political figures and parties within the government enables parts of the FIS program to be coopted by other political parties and programs, whittling away at any FIS monopoly of a regime critique; under these circumstances, the FIS will more rapidly assume the position of a "normal" party with a much smaller following than the plurality it gained in 1991.

- After other political parties have succeeded in establishing their own foothold on the political scene, the FIS too would be legitimized, as long as it was not *directly* linked to political violence.

The main problem with this more optimistic scenario is that it requires an army that is willing to relinquish power in general terms to a political process that is not controllable and predictable. There is no reason to think that the army is at this stage, or that Zerwal wishes to go in this direction. Zerwal more likely seeks to maintain a firm ban on the FIS and to maintain a basically autocratic government that makes gestures to other non-FIS parties or figures to fulfill the minimal requirements for legitimacy in the eyes of the domestic and foreign public. Zerwal, therefore, will evolve a political order more typical of Egypt—nominally pluralistic, but in reality still fairly tightly controlled by a variety of administrative means, methods of cooption, selected police oppression, etc.

In the end, the case can be made that most of Algeria and the external world simply wants a modicum of order and prosperity, free of gross abuses of human rights by the state. A stable and prosperous Algeria is of course very desirable. But the calculus that the Islamists can be systematically denied access to the political order over the longer run will not be a healthy one. For only their participation will bring them into a state of "normalcy" within the political order, in which the public no longer sees them as having any "magic Islamic answers" to pressing questions of the day. Furthermore, the chances are very good that a majority of states in the region will not be successful in managing the daunting economic, social, and political issues that are building. As long as they do not, the Islamists—especially if they are excluded from power—will be the primary beneficiaries of these failing policies. Islamists included in the political agony and search for appropriate policies will be less able to routinely exploit national crises with simplistic slogans. Nor can it be completely ruled out that the Islamists will not have anything to offer in the national search for answers—especially in the area of social policy, in which they have had some success in the poorer communities.

Sant' Egidio has never been accepted by the regime. Is it therefore now a dead letter?

A DEMOCRATIC RESOLUTION

If the army high command will relent, a second, democratic, solution could emerge through a return to an electoral process. The stakes for both the army and the FIS are high in such a process. The military runs the risk of sanctioning a FIS plurality in the next elections. It will then be less able to overturn the results again, or to reassert military rule against the FIS, without drawing renewed international criticism and rekindling harsh civil conflict.

There would be much to say for a FIS-led government in a coalition with several other political parties. It would launch the country into a democratic experiment in which all parties—including the FIS—would be forced to compromise on their maximum agenda. Algeria is fortunate that it, unlike Egypt, still has several other vibrant and credible political parties with significant followings that could help moderate any FIS tendencies toward extremism. And the FIS would be required to recognize the limitations placed upon it by the popular will.[18]

There is nothing about this exercise in democratic procedure and governance that offers any certain formula for success. Such a coalition government could easily become deadlocked, descending into impotence, public disillusionment, and ultimately a return to the politics of the street—typical of the pattern of many fledgling democracies. But it has the advantage of containing the most radical urges of the FIS at the time when it first enters government, it forces the FIS

---

[18]The importance of the precise *mechanics* of an electoral process—highlighted in Algeria's ill-fated 1991 elections, ostensibly stacked by the FLN in its own favor—cannot be overemphasized; systems of weighting, proportionality, thresholds of participation, and many other mechanical procedures can play a major role in containing the behavior of small radical parties, or, conversely, weakening potentially robust government. Successive governments of Italy over the decades were hamstrung by complex coalition formulas designed expressly to dilute Communist Party strength and keep it from gaining a majority.

to compromise with other groups and to expose its own thinking to the moderating influence of others, and will allow the electorate to decide whether next time it wants more—or less—of what the FIS can do. Today, FIS slogans and principles provide the public little basis for predicting how it will function in office.

A third, transitional scenario might envisage a continuing weakening of the army and the regime under continuing military and guerrilla conflict, with the FIS coming to gain control of major regions of the country that the military could not successfully contest. In this situation, the country would be divided indefinitely, warring sporadically, until one or another faction was exhausted and willing to reach a political compromise. Unfortunately, it seems to be a characteristic of Algerian political culture that it is not greatly given to compromise.

A final scenario involves a prolongation of the present situation in which the junta is unable to reach out to other parties or even to dominate the country militarily and suppress the Islamists, nor are the Islamists able to dislodge the military hold on the basic instruments of power. Such a stalemate could continue for quite some time. Ultimately, however, this scenario has to give way to the collapse of one faction or the other, and the Islamic radicals do not seem likely to collapse entirely. The regime would be dangerously exposed to a disillusioned and unsupportive public; unfortunately, the country is well versed in the tactics of urban guerrilla warfare from the late 1950s in the struggle against the French.[19]

---

[19]The classic 1965 film about the Algerian revolution, *The Battle of Algiers,* in its portrayal of urban warfare against the French, today reflects in an eerie way the kinds of techniques the FIS is now using against the ruling junta.

Chapter Eight

IMPLICATIONS FOR THE UNITED STATES

The United States is not a major player in the Algerian situation; Algeria historically has belonged to the realm of special French interest and involvement. U.S. concern and consultation with allies has been propelled primarily by the gravity of the situation, and its broader regional implications. While France will undoubtedly be the state most singly affected by a negative course of events in Algeria, the crisis has other important effects:

- It affects the stability of Morocco, with which the United States has close ties, Tunisia, with which the United States has good ties, and even Egypt, which plays a central role in U.S. interests in the Middle East. Instability in North Africa increasingly stirs concern among U.S. allies in Europe who fear instability across the Mediterranean, the possible flight of large numbers of refugees, the exportation of internal Algerian terrorism into Europe, and the impact upon the energy supplies to European states in the southern Mediterranean.

- The United States is concerned about the impact of Algerian Islamist movements upon the broader issue of Islamist movements across the Muslim world.

- Security threats to Europe from the south affect the NATO alliance and place additional pressure upon NATO's already hard-pressed southern command to develop yet new abilities for coping with eastern Mediterranean crises.

- The United States has a further interest in the development of a distinctive Mediterranean security structure that can cope precisely with such problems as an Algerian crisis.

In practical terms, the United States needs to maintain close consultation with Morocco and Tunisia on the course of the Algerian crisis—Morocco in particular, because it has been far more skillful and imaginative in dealing with its own domestic Islamist groups than Tunisia has. Advanced discussion and planning are also required to anticipate problems and responses that could stem from a breakdown of order in Algeria or the elevation of FIS to power, particularly by extraconstitutional means. This kind of planning needs to anticipate potential FIS support to Islamist movements in the neighboring countries and its implications, as well as refugee problems or pipeline security problems.

The United States will need to remain realistic about the fact that Islamist movements generally are not "exported" so much as they are "imported." Where political, social, and economic conditions are ripe, an openness, a vulnerability, even an ideological "need" will exist that welcomes the catalyst that an Islamic movement and ideology can provide. While funding and weapons from abroad can often make an important difference to a local movement, the essence of the problem exists at home. It is precisely in these terms, then, that we need to recognize the FIS as a "legitimate" political challenger that springs from local historical conditions and needs and will not go away simply because it is threatening to the local regime or even foreign interests. It is not a "cancer" that can be excised from the body politic.

Second, the United States faces a complex conceptual problem of stability versus change in the region. While the dilemma is theoretical—and in every case will be different—the reality is that there are a large number of states in the Middle East in which change is long overdue in the political, economic, and social spheres. Policies simply designed to "keep the lid on" will usually have the effect of delaying the reforms and changes that are essential to heading off more severe political convulsions later. Of course every country will have its own unique dynamic that requires separate treatment. But the broader problem must be recognized if sufficient weight is to be given to the need for introducing change. It is tempting to support authoritarian solutions over the short term as long as there are no explosions. But such authoritarian solutions are not likely to resolve any underlying problems, nor are the problems likely to go away in the meantime.

Third, most regimes in the region are likely to plead with the United States about the need for relief from human rights requirements and political reforms as long as they are confronted by "Islamic fundamentalist terrorism." These regimes indeed seek to ensure that their Islamist challengers can be tarred with the "terrorist" brush by using violent repression to push them into violent response—as has been very much the case in Algeria and Egypt. The presence of "radical fundamentalism" serves as a permanent alibi for regime reluctance or failure to bring about reform. Indeed, Washington will be the key target for such campaigns of persuasion, by regimes that believe it will retreat from its principles out of fear of the fundamentalist threat. There is no simple answer, but policymakers need to remain deeply aware of the character of this generic dilemma and avoid entrapment in it. Islamist movements, in short, will represent in many ways the vehicle, the cutting edge, of demand for political and economic reform at the mass level, especially when regimes seek to eliminate most other political parties as well. Often only Islamists then survive such repression, because they work through mosque networks rather than through formal parties.

Indeed, there is a considerable likelihood that a new wave of authoritarianism in the region will take the form of an alliance of Middle Eastern regimes united to protect their own power and status quo, enlisting each other and the West in the grander project of fighting "terrorism" and "fundamentalism." Thus, while terrorism should of course be a concern of the West as well as of the region, it is important that facile labels such as "terrorism" and "fundamentalism" be carefully examined before they push the United States into strong stands against native movements that threaten existing, usually unconstitutional, regimes that seek Western support.

In this sense, it is valuable for the United States, in conjunction with its European allies—and perhaps with Russia—to develop an understanding of the dynamic of Islamist movements and a set of working principles on how to approach the problem. Until this understanding exists, various state policies may find it difficult to formulate principles in response to the Islamic challenge on an ad hoc basis.

Fourth, the Algerian crisis raises broad and complex issues of Mediterranean security as a whole. Issues of development in the Maghreb affect a broad range of European and Western interests; the Maghreb's economic development has direct impact on its employment levels, pressures for emigration to Europe, emigration policy, broader trading issues such as preferential trade policies for the Maghreb, regional trade policies, energy policies, investment in the Maghreb, human rights concerns, and others. The European Community has come to the realization that it needs to develop a systematic European policy toward the Maghreb, one that takes a long-term interest in the evolution of these states, right on Europe's doorstep, which can no longer be kept at arm's length.

Fifth, short of much greater deterioration of the situation in Algeria, and evidence of a general European inability to cope with the problem, the stakes are not so high as to justify significant U.S. intervention. But the prevention of civil war and the attainment of a political solution in Algeria is unquestionably an important goal for the United States. This study argues that it is equally important to support a political solution that in some way ameliorates the destabilizing character of the FIS and brings it into the political system. Such a solution will potentially have a major impact upon the course of political Islam in the region as a whole. Indeed, the way the FIS is handled will have a major impact on the way the FIS conducts itself in some kind of eventual role in government. It is not in the U.S. interest—nor that of the region—for the FIS to be rigorously and illegally excluded from participation in the political process or from governance if it maintains power at the polls. A FIS that perceives itself as *excluded by definition* as a political party—with the collusion of the West—simply because it is Islamist, will be a dangerous force within the body politic that will likely help to perpetuate violence and extremism in Algerian politics. Only through participation in the political process, too, will the FIS come under the scrutiny of the general public; it will then have the opportunity to demonstrate what it can and cannot do, thereby strongly affecting its base of political support. The author believes that a FIS exposed to the political process will in the end lose much of its previous mass support and will be reduced to much more modest levels of popular support.

If the FIS is likely to gain an eventual voice in government, it is imperative that it come only through established, agreed-upon institutionalized procedure, rather than through collapse of an autocratic regime or a solution imposed by violence or anarchy. It is not in the power of either the United States or France to micromanage the transition from an unconstitutional junta to constitutional procedures, but an effort to stimulate and encourage such a process is imperative. We are talking about not just one country, but the future development of the Islamist phenomenon in much of the Muslim world. These movements are potentially given to extremism, but do not automatically have to go the route of Iran—or even Sudan.

The attainment of power by legal means suggests strong constraints exerted by the discipline that constitutions, democracy, and due process are all supposed to impose. This process just might encourage the possibility of Islamists relinquishing power by the same electoral process if defeated—as indeed the FIS claims it will do through recognition of the principle of political power alternation.

One might object that the argument of Islamist inclusion in the political process resembles earlier arguments in the Cold War about the handling of communist parties as well—sworn enemies of democratic procedure. Two responses are relevant. One, the phenomenon of communists coming to power in local or regional elections in many parts of the world was an acceptable, not even alarming process (such as in Italy and India), where local communist administration was nothing exceptional nor particularly risky. Second, communism had an ideological and power center in the Soviet Union (or China). The spread of communist rule was a direct gain for the USSR, one of two poles in a bipolar world order. Islamism is nothing like this—with no center, no Islamintern, no clear international policy line, no predictable bloc of states, no certain program. Islamist politics flow directly from the local traditional culture. Finally, Islamist movements present considerable diversity, and the antidemocratic principle is not automatically inherent in them. They are furthermore evolving over time—although not all in equally desirable directions.

It is important that Islamist political movements and ideas be tried and tested if the public wants to test them. And that is just the point—*if* the public wants to test them. Only in this way will Islamist policies be seen for what they are: a range of movements from utopian radicalism, native forms of authoritarianism, conservative social movements, or even social movements that just might address some specific social needs effectively, but not others. Only experience with political Islam will begin to deflate the phenomenon and allow it to find its proper modest level on the political spectrum. Otherwise, if Islamism by definition is denied access to political power, it becomes more radicalized, and frustrated publics feel somehow that maybe Islam is indeed "the answer." Only experience will demystify it. The more that Islamism is imposed—by war, revolution, or coup—the less the chance that it will be seen for what it is, and the more radical the form it will take under anarchistic circumstances of assuming power.

So far, the record of Islamist governance is not encouraging in Iran and Sudan. But the political phenomenon is still young and evolving. It has not come to power yet via constitutional means. Harsh conditions will produce radical ideologies. Where behavior from Islamist regimes is unacceptable on the international level, sanctions will have to be taken by the global community to constrict or isolate such regimes. What is unrealistic is the hope that we can entirely avoid Islamism's entering the political process.

In the final analysis, the FIS is quite likely to remain a major even if not dominant force in Algerian politics. It may even come to power, either in the face of a government breakdown or by some sort of compromise:

- A FIS victory by government collapse or by military means is the most undesirable situation, since a revolutionary victory only encourages the most radical forces to take power. Under such circumstances there will be no moderating constraints upon the FIS, making it less likely that it will rule democratically.

- A back-room nondemocratic deal on power sharing has the advantage of occurring within controlled guidelines. Its main drawback is that it provides less legitimacy to the resulting regime, and makes further violation of any democratic procedure easier in the future. The FIS has so far said it will not engage in any power-sharing nondemocratic deal with the army.

- An agreement could be reached by all the political parties over the head of the regime—resembling the Sant' Egidio agreements. Such a solution would require strong Western support for the Sant' Egidio parties to impose it upon the current junta. But as long as the junta offers promise of moving toward a more open democratic process after the (scarcely representative) presidential elections of November 1995, the West is not likely to pressure Algiers in this direction. Should the junta fail to move toward dialog and democratization, however, this kind of a solution remains an important consideration. The FIS would, of course, play a major but not totally dominant role in such a process.

- The most desirable process is for the FIS to demonstrate its own political strength at the polls in new elections; but will the junta agree?

All of these solutions posit that the FIS will come to participate in power in some form eventually; the task then becomes how to craft a process that will do the most to preserve Algeria's stability, promote an open political order, and limit the power of radicals to turn the state to their own ideological ends.

The United States is capable of helping manage this process, perhaps by working with its European allies, especially France, to set forth a proposed set of procedures whereby a return to democratic policy can take place—especially in the event that the junta is unable to move in the right direction. A European accord on the issue will basically give the FIS a great deal of what it wants by way of reopening the door to democratic process. Such an accord also lends a solemnity and internationally monitored institutional character to that electoral process, which will make it harder, but certainly not impossible, for the FIS later to renege on prolongation of democracy in subsequent elections—even at the cost of losing.

U.S. policy should also be marked by principle, i.e., above all the need to establish electoral procedures in Algeria—even at the risk that the FIS will win a dominant voice in government by gaining a plurality of votes. U.S. policy should not be driven by a goal to prevent the FIS from gaining a major voice in government—especially when it involves perversion of democratic process. To do so sends the wrong message to the region and will delay the process of Islamist politics coming into contact with the reality of governance. That experience cannot likely be staved off; to try to do so will only increase violence and delay the process whereby political Islam loses its special status and falls into "normal political perspective" in the region.

*   *   *

Given the magnitude of the problems, the FIS in power will probably not demonstrate remarkable success in areas where its predecessors have failed. But it is bound to have some new ideas, at least in terms of community services, new social programs, the weeding out of egregious corruption, possibly the restoration of some sense of community, and perhaps even to broaden the basis of public participation in the governing process beyond what it has been to date. But even here, where these FIS approaches conceivably might be positive, they almost surely will be insufficient to the task of managing the massive social challenges before the state.

The FIS itself will almost surely come to experience the pressures of failure in not being able to resolve these complex issues. Disillusionment could then break out among its followers. At that point, the FIS stands at a major crossroads. Will it attempt then to broaden the system—as the FLN once should have done—and bring in domestic expertise wherever it can be found? Or will it revert to classical suppression of its opponents and a narrowing and tightening of the system, replacing secular tyranny with Islamic tyranny? Once a potential FIS tyranny is in place, the long journey back once again will have to traverse the same painful road it did with the FLN—rioting, violence, and conflict until the system is once again opened up by some new counterforce.

Either path is fateful for the region. An Islamist regime that is able to adjust to reality, and pragmatically open itself to society in order to draw in maximum political talent, will be a major step forward in the annals of Islamic governance. Such an event would suggest that Islamist politics too, are capable of evolution and progress in the region. But to retrace the same, dreary authoritarian path trodden by so many other Middle Eastern regimes of different ideological stripes will only be further convincing evidence that the Islamist approach to reform and governance has nothing to offer. Islam as a religion will then have taken one more step in the direction of relegation to the sphere of private faith and piety rather than an operative political concept. The stakes are high—most of all for Algeria, but also for the region, for the West's relationship with it, and for the future of political Islam.

BIBLIOGRAPHY

Addi, Lahouari, "Islam politique et democratization en Algerie," *Esprit*, August 1992.

B., Fatima, "Algeria's Veil of Tears," *Freedom Review*, May–June 1994.

Bekkar, Rabia, "Taking up Space in Tlemcen: The Islamist Occupation of Urban Algeria," *Middle East Report*, November–December 1992.

————, "The Shrinking Space of Algerian Politics," *Freedom Review*, Vol. 23, No. 3, 1994.

Belkacem, Cherif, "Le FIS: algerien avant tout," *Jeune Afrique*, January 9, 1992.

Burgat, Francois, and William McDowell, *The Islamic Movement in North Africa*, Center for Middle East Studies, The University of Texas at Austin, 1993.

Carlier, Omar, "De l'islahisme a l'islamisme: la therapie politico-religieuse du FIS," *Cahiers d'Etudes africaines*, #2, 1992.

Cheriet, Boutheina, "Islamism and Feminism," in John C. Entelis and Phillip C. Naylor (eds.), *State and Society in Algeria*, Boulder, CO: Westview, 1992.

De La Gorce, Paul-Marie, "Le joker des Islamistes," *Jeune Afrique*, January 9, 1992.

————, "Voyage au coeur de l'armee," *Jeune Afrique*, April 21, 1994.

Demir, Mehmet, "Human Rights Briefing," *Middle East Report,* November–December 1992, pp. 38–39.

Dillman, Bradford, "Transition to Democracy in Algeria," in John C. Entelis and Phillip C. Naylor (eds.), *State and Society in Algeria,* Boulder, CO: Westview, 1992.

Entelis, John C., "Political Islam in Algeria: The Non-violent Dimension," *Current History,* January 1995.

———, "Islam, Democracy, and the State: The Reemergence of Authoritarian Politics in Algeria," in John Ruedy (ed.), *Islamism and Secularism in North Africa,* New York: St. Martin's Press, 1994.

Entelis, John C., and Phillip C. Naylor (eds.), *State and Society in Algeria,* Boulder, CO: Westview, 1992.

Jansen, G. H., *Militant Islam,* London: Pan Books, 1979.

Kaid, Hamza, "Le Drapeau des Islamistes flottera-t-il sur l'Algerie?" *Jeune Afrique,* January 9, 1992.

Kapil, Arun, "Algeria's Elections Show Islamist Strength," *Middle East Report,* September–October 1990.

Kaplan, Roger, "The War for Algeria," *Freedom Review,* May–June 1994.

Al-Kenz, Ali, *Algerian Reflections on Arab Crises,* Robert W. Stookey (trans.), Austin: University of Texas Press, 1991.

Kusserov, Mourad, "Islam in Algeria: Past—and Future?" *Swiss Review of World Affairs,* April 1994.

Leveau, Remy, *Algeria: Adversaries in Search of Uncertain Compromises,* Chaillot Paper 4, Paris: Institute for Security Studies, Western European Union, September 1992.

———, *Le Sabre et Le Turban: L'avenir du Maghreb,* Paris: Editions Francois Bourin, 1993.

Middle East Economic Digest.

Middle East Report, November–December 1992, pp. 9–13.

Mideast Mirror, "Akhbar al-Khaleej: What's Holding up the National Dialog?" June 2, 1994.

Mileb, Najib, "Algerie: l'impossible victoire de l'armee," *Jeune Afrique,* July 22, 1993.

Mimouni, Rachid, *The Honor of the Tribe,* Joachim Neugroschel (trans.), New York: William Morrow and Company, 1989.

Mortimer, Robert, "Islam and Multiparty Politics in Algeria," *The Middle East Journal,* Autumn 1991.

Radu, Michael, "Islam and Politics in Black Africa," *Dissent,* Summer 1992.

Randal, Jonathan C., "Islamic Front Steps Up Struggle in Algeria," *Washington Post,* June 6, 1994.

Roberts, Hugh, "A Trial of Strength: Algerian Islamism," in James Piscatori (ed.), *Islamic Fundamentalisms and the Gulf Crisis,* Chicago: American Academy of Arts and Sciences, 1991.

———, "Algeria Between Eradicators and Conciliators," *Middle East Report,* July–August 1994.

Roy, Olivier, *The Failure of Political Islam,* Carol Volk (trans.), Cambridge, MA: Harvard University Press, 1994.

Ruedy, John, *Modern Algeria,* Bloomington: Indiana University Press, 1992.

Singer, Daniel, "Algeria Slides Into Civil War," *The Nation,* February 21, 1994.

Soudan, Francois, "Les Islamistes peuvent-ils gagner?: Maghreb," *Jeune Afrique,* July 22, 1993.

Swearingen, Will D., "Algeria's Food Security Crisis," *Middle East Report,* September–October 1990.

Tlemcani, Rachid, "Chadli's Perestroika," *Middle East Report,* November–December 1992, pp. 14–17.

Yared, Marc, "La deuxieme guerre d'Algerie a-t-elle commence?" *Jeune Afrique,* August 1, 1992.

————, "Egypte: La Misere contre l'etat," *Jeune Afrique*, July 22, 1993.

Youssefi, Mohamed, "Algerie: D'une guerre a l'autre," *Jeune Afrique*, April 7, 1994.